"A very enthusiastic and plain-spoken book that celebrates the author's lifelong love affair with poetry . . . lyrical."
— *The Baltimore Sun*

"Molly Peacock's reassuring words are a perfect balm for National Poetry Month. . . . Simple, straightforward help that gives the fearful a five-minutes-a-day introduction to poetry, the intermediate reader the inspiration to 'fall in love' with poetry, and the courageous a guide to starting a poetry circle with friends."
— *St. Louis Post-Dispatch*

"In a successful effort to demonstrate the value of her oft-neglected medium, poet and memoirist Molly Peacock guides the reader through thirteen of her favorite poems with grace, humor, and warmth. . . . Her sheer delight in them is infectious. . . . Essential for poetry novices yet thoroughly enjoyable for initiates, this illuminating handbook is a joy."
— *Kirkus Reviews*

"Peacock provides a simple yet elegant template for reading poetry. . . . Eschewing a literary context for a psychological focus, Peacock offers formal yet personal readings of poems by a dozen poets, including Jane Kenyon, May Swenson, Michael Ondaatje, Margaret Atwood, and the eleventh-century Chinese poet Li Ch'ing-chao. These lovely selections and her lucid interpretations provide a welcoming introduction to the art of reading poetry, and her suggestions for forming a poetry circle are meant to encourage poem-struck readers to articulate and share their passion."
— *Booklist*

(continued on next page . . .)

ALSO BY MOLLY PEACOCK

And Live Apart

Raw Heaven

Take Heart

Original Love

Paradise, Piece by Piece

COEDITOR

Poetry in Motion:
100 Poems from the Subways and Buses

RIVERHEAD

BOOKS

a

member

of

RIVERHEAD

BOOKS

New York

1999

How

to

Read

a

Poem . . .

and

Start

a

Poetry

Circle

MOLLY PEACOCK

Most Riverhead Books are available at special quantity discounts for bulk purchases for sales promotions, premiums, fund-raising or educational use. Special books, or book excerpts, can also be created to fit specific needs.

For details, write: Special Markets, The Berkley Publishing Group, 375 Hudson Street, New York, NY 10014.

Riverhead Books
Published by The Berkley Publishing Group
A division of Penguin Putnam Inc.
375 Hudson Street
New York, New York 10014

A list of permissions appears on pages 208–9.

First Riverhead hardcover edition: April 1999
First Riverhead trade paperback edition: March 2000
Riverhead trade paperback ISBN: 1-57322-785-4

The Penguin Putnam Inc. World Wide Web site address is
http: //www.penguinputnam.com

The Library of Congress has catalogued
the Riverhead hardcover edition as follows:

Peacock, Molly.
How to read a poem—and start a poetry circle / by Molly Peacock.
p.   cm.
ISBN 1-57322-128-7
1. Poetry.   I. Title.
PN1031.P358 1999   98-55132 CIP
818.1—dc21

PRINTED IN THE UNITED STATES OF AMERICA

10   9   8   7   6   5   4   3   2   1

For my teachers:
Mrs. Knowlton, Mrs. Baeumler,
Milton Kessler & Richard Howard

If you have form'd a circle to go into,
Go into it yourself, and see how you would do.

WILLIAM BLAKE

from "Gnomic Verses ii: To God"

Contents

How

to

Read

a

Poem . . .

and

Start

a

Poetry

Circle

CHAPTER ONE

The Letter O . . . Talismans . . . Teachers . . . A Calling . . . And Friends

The Letter O . . .

When I first fell in love with the word "joy," because it had a circle inside it, I did not know I was entering a whole way of life. I noticed that while nothing prevented *o* from appearing at beginnings and endings of words, it was a bigger, rounder O if it lay in the middle, as it does in *love* or *world*. Inevitably, as *joy* led to *love*, *world* led me to the word. I still did not realize I had found a method of being through an impulsive rapture with the fifteenth letter of the alphabet, or even that I had passed through the open gates of a wooded community that, while it wasn't a secret, did seem to have a password: poetry.

A circle, the O of a mouth, holding hands, a hula hoop,

a halo, and later in life, the aure*o*le of a breast, an *o*rgasm . . . That O was a connector of all things, and it linked me to a habit of thinking—and sanctioned a way of feeling—my way through life among others who have also felt intensely and thought deeply. These are the readers of poetry. The childhood world that led to the word also led me to teachers, to friends, and finally to a strangely easy compatibility with ambiguity—that is to say, the mystery of adult life. Poetry guided me to and through love affairs, toward friendships, into marriage, and to my own vocation.

While at first I was astonished to find that the word "circle" has no *o* in it, I also felt the curious combination of being both delighted and stymied that I came to identify with reading poetry. To be comfortable with many inexplicable meanings, yet to be able to find meaning, to actively locate it in a syllable, a beat, an image, and to have clarity and mystery at the same time—that seems to define the complete way to live. Whatever poetry does, it is always tuned to paradoxes. Of course, I had to admit that poetry was becoming my religion. Inside the word "religion"—and also tucked inside a more bodily word, "ligament"—is the Latin root *ligare*, meaning to connect, to bind fast. I was connected not only to poems but to other people who have read them.

. . . *Talismans* . . .

Each time any of us reads a favorite poem, it conjures a special sorcery of second sight, and third, and fourth, until understanding is so profound that we are returned to a state before we even had language—a prelinguistic place. That's why it is so hard to say exactly what a poem means. Like being stupidly in love, this art leaves you dumbstruck. Yet how rare—and thrilling—to be struck dumb in the all too articulate world.

At first I was enthralled by certain tall, mysterious poems. Then some ordinary-looking poems that turned out to be great dancers captured me. Some poems don't dance at all. They speak to you from deep inside their chairs, and you know that you are forming a friendship with them that will last your whole life. By giving me passionate reading experiences, these poems taught me how to use intensity, and I discovered a personal mythology in my relationship with each of them. I built stories around them—and found new choices.

But as I was afraid of love, I could be afraid of my poems. After all, attempting to understand them sometimes feels like entering a maelstrom. Many people who feel a tentative affinity to poetry—even love it, and sometimes even write it—don't really feel they understand it. Slowly I discovered that the apprehension of a poem is a sensuous mental activity. And understanding is gained just the way a love relationship is deepened—through the blind delight of examining it with the senses and the intellect all at once. Emotive brainwork creates luxurious understanding.

Sometimes I think we are attracted to a poem because it makes us feel as if someone is listening to us. This may seem like a strange reversal, because we are supposed to be listening to *it*, but the voice of the poem allows us to hear ourselves. It can be a great comfort to hear our own voices emanating through the letters of words that come from someone else. But it can also produce confusion, because we do not always allow ourselves to hear our inner voice and are alarmed by its sound. That is why we say our poets speak *for* us. Certain poems allow you to feel what you mean, even though you cannot dare to say what that is yourself.

Our sense inarticulacy in the face of the most articulate art, a helplessness in its presence—coupled with a sureness of our attachment to it *even though we don't know why*—can bewitch us. Or at least it has bewitched me. I've stood shifting from foot to foot, in classrooms, in bookstores, in boudoirs, puzzling through poetry's conundrums all my reading life. When we hear our forbidden inner natures inside the rhythm of another—as when I heard *Our fate is forked* in the voice of an anonymous medieval poet, or *Pitched past pitch of grief* in Gerard Manley Hopkins' voice, or even in the twentieth-century voice of Elizabeth Bishop, in the line *Somebody loves us all*—we may encounter an aspect of a poem that refuses insight, and seems to be untranslatable into our own internal language. This might be due to psychological resistance, or to the sudden distance between bodily and intellectual understanding. This toughness of resistance to meaning feels as if the poem had an impenetrable rind—yet how the poem glows! And through that rind a light shines out to us, and these poems become our talismans.

A talisman is an object that gives its bearer a special hold on life, even though the talisman itself might at first be as undecipherable as an ancient Chinese poem written in ideograms. But a hold on life is what I got from my favorite poems, and I tote them around like amulets against the world, using them to ward off every evil. The Greek root *telesma* means a consecration, a fulfillment, or complete, and my talisman poems have a holy quality of sensuous pleasure.

. . . *Teachers* . . .

After a while it occurred to me that I could make these amulets myself. I first made one as a girl, when I was ten, then another a few years later, then a group of haiku in high school. I felt so secretive about them that I wrote in French—bad, halting French. Nor was I one of those kids who wrote in lockable leather notebooks. Instead, I would write something on a bit of paper, enjoying the fact that the paper was free on all four sides, unbound. Then I'd tote it around for years, just the way I did the talismans I read. I took the most pleasure in writing and reading small portable things, so I liked short musical poems, lyric poetry. Figuring out how to make lyric poems made me read better. After all, I had to understand the model in order to repeat it and make it my own. That was when I began taking such poems apart, the way some boys I knew dismantled clocks. We all were interested in how things ticked.

A few times when I took a poem apart, it never came back together again. Inadvertently I had become the bully who tears the wings from butterflies. I would rather not understand than kill a poem, I resolved right then, and looked to my teachers for help. They took literature apart all the time. My third-grade teacher, Mrs. Knowlton, made me love school at a time when everything was falling apart at home. I had developed my lifelong insomnia, waking up at night to creep to the top of the stairs and listen to the words my parents were screaming at each other below. They were like dragons thrashing. I needed something to protect myself. School became an amulet—though it was hardly the kind of thing you could put in your pocket. I don't remember reading or writing poems with Mrs. Knowlton. It was the quality of her attention that moved me, similar to that inverted sense of being listened to by a poem, even though *you* are listening to *it*. Even though Mrs. Knowlton was doing most of the talking, as a poem does, I felt acknowledged, perhaps even *discovered*. When we discover poems, they seem to rediscover us. She was teaching me how to read better, more subtly. And because of it I felt more subtly defined. Isn't it felicitous that the word "know" is inside Mrs. *Know*lton? (And inside ac*know*ledge . . .)

My mother and I thought Mrs. Knowlton was a spinster, even though we were supposed to call her Mrs. After all, she wore no makeup and she alternated two wool suits, one heather, the other gray. But one day we read in the *Buffalo Courier Express* that she and her husband had bought an old hearse, fixed it up as a camper, and gone to Mexico for the summer. Mrs. Knowlton was an adventurer! She had poetry in her soul—and a husband, too. I wrote her a letter. And she wrote back from Mexico. Of course, the next year was dreadful without her. But I was still attached to school, because of how her teaching defined me, or let me begin to define myself.

I waited years for another one of these experiences, until my seventh-grade teacher Mrs. Baeumler introduced me to Keats. I wrote my first grown-up poem, published in *Silver Voices: the twenty-fifth anthology of original verse by the boys and girls of the Kenmore Public Schools*. Mrs. Baeumler sent it in for me. "Balmy" was thin and blonde. We called her that because we all thought she had to be crazy to pay so much attention to twelve-year-olds. For extra credit she would wave her long hand like a delphinium toward the half-shelf of hard-core adult poetry in the school library. As a Beginning French student, I translated "La Belle Dame Sans Merci" as "The Bell-Shaped Woman Without Thank You." I had rashly decided never ever to apologize for anything I did—and I looked for a like spirit in the woman who wouldn't say thanks. I didn't really find one, but I also didn't *not* find one, as Philip Larkin in his poem "Talking in Bed" looks for *Words at once true and kind,/Or not untrue and not unkind*.

I found grown-up poetry to be as spongy as a forest floor—your foot sinks into the pine needles, the air smells mushroomy and dank, and filtered light swirls around you till you're deep in another state. Since the tobacco-and-violet-scented Balmy announced that no one's opinion about verse was ever wrong, I gleefully entered the woods of interpretation. It was all right to be lost.

My next teacher made me so mad I've forgotten his name. He specialized in instruments of torture: dactyls, antistrophes, similes, and quatrains. The classroom had mental dead insect bodies all over the floor, diaphanous wings ripped from Wordsworth and Shakespeare. I'd never understood these poets to begin with, and now all the shine of their life was gone. Poetry and teachers were intertwined for me, and if the teacher wasn't alive, then the poems had no *duende*, the word Federico García Lorca uses for the great devilish spirit in poems.

The older I got, the greater my need for talismans be-came—and the greater my enchantment with the sexy strangers of poetry. (What we hold sacred is often related to our bodies.) At Binghamton University, which everyone knew as Harpur College then, poetry began to drape my life in the sensuous fabric of adulthood. I fell in love with my poetry professor, of course. Milton Kessler was a real poet who had the sense to leave poems whole even as he inves-tigated them. He was like a marvelous, magnetic, intense field biologist, capturing, examining—but never interfer-ing. With consummate kindness he left me on my own, smiling at whatever specimens I brought to him. He made me want to reacquaint myself with the Linnaean-like clas-sifications of verse I once had thought were instruments of torture. Now, words like "meter" and "prosody" made me curious—like the Latin terms for sex organs.

Each time I understood a poem better, I made some de-cision in my own life that I understood better than before—because poems showed me unvarnished states of human emotion that I could examine. After many decades, I real-ized that art was the healthiest part of my life, and if I could make mature decisions in life the way I made them in art, with the concentration, focus, and balanced energy of po-etry, then I would be leading a life I admired.

It took me a while to know what kind of life that was. I married and divorced. Meanwhile, I had completely buried a love I had for my high school and college boyfriend, a man I had lost touch with, but found and married nineteen years later. During our time away from each other, he became a scholar, devoting himself to literature. I had worked as a college administrator and even published a number of poems before I realized I had to get back to school—to learn more about *ars poetica*. At The Johns Hopkins University I met Richard Howard—poet, critic, and translator—who charged poetry in ways that electrified me. He wore the windy robes of vocabulary, lined with the silks of etymology, gusseted with pockets for stray linguistic facts. This delighted me as if my own uncle had appeared with shiny gifts from abroad. But compared to Richard's, my words felt plain as fenceposts. Here was a man of letters. And I was a woman of . . . What *was* I a woman of?

I wasn't a scholar. I knew I didn't have the temperament for it, as I learned from another Johns Hopkins figure, the art historian and poet Michael Fried. Fried shimmered with enthusiasm over the same poems I knew and loved— they were *his* talismans, too! But there was nothing he adored more than being buried in the stacks of a library for hours into days into months. And I wanted to be out in the world. But where in the world *was* that world?

. . . *A Calling* . . .

By now the double helix of teaching and poetry had entered me, yet I didn't want to be a professor. I couldn't declare myself a woman of letters—that was probably something one became in spite of oneself, not by trying. I was blessed by those who taught me poetry, triply blessed by the fact that all respected and attended to me as if I were a special species of plant. Still, their goals seemed mapped, and I was inventing a life. Slowly I realized that a literary life for me would involve writing poems, reading poems—and teaching the talismans I was still avidly collecting. It was then that I realized my talismans had actually collected *me*. Now I know they are so interrelated that they make a strange kind of sacred and profane family of poems. They are about God and sex and defining a self, and these, not surprisingly, are concerns in my own poetry.

To learn about something hair-triggered and complex, complete with its own structures and therefore its own ways of knowing and conveying, is to illumine the paths of existence itself. Communing with these poems collected over years, each continuing to exhibit vitality as I look at its body—its nervous system, skeletal system, circulatory system—with greater consciousness and greater regard, fires in me a respect for the conscious act of living. And that is what I hope to convey when I teach people how to read a poem.

. . .

Each chapter of this book introduces one or two of my talisman poems, and tells the story of how it came to be so,
and shows some of the many ways we can enter a poem and
understand it. I begin with a recent amulet, by a poet I
knew, Jane Kenyon, but then I revisit one of my early favorites, an poem more than a thousand years old that was
written by an anonymous medieval woman. Then she is
joined by another thousand-year-old poem from halfway
across her world, by the eleventh-century Chinese poet Li
Ch'ing-chao. The poems are sometimes well known, like
Gerard Manley Hopkins' sonnet "No Worst" or Philip
Larkin's "Talking in Bed," and are sometimes more obscure,
like the Romantic poet John Clare's "I Am." Clare's poem
sits in the same mental niche as Marilyn Nelson's poem of
jealousy in a women's locker room. Michael Ondaatje's
poem of his father's letters shares a shelf with Yusef Komunyakaa's poem about *his* father's letters. Another of my
favorites, Elizabeth Bishop's poem "Filling Station," for example, I love as an emblem of all her work, as I do May
Swenson's "Question." Even one of my own poems, "The
Fare," has become a talisman for me—a poem I always hope
would make my mother laugh if she were still alive.

The resurgence of poetry now, when a decade ago some
were pronouncing it dead as a genre, does have everything
to do with time, even though talisman poems seem to stop
time. In a cybermoment when quickness is everything (and

it is nice to remember that to quicken means to enliven, that the Book of Common Prayer calls the living "the quick"), poetry, the screen-size art, provides depth. It is both brief and profound. Our hunger is for levels of meaning, but our need is instant. Poetry is the art that offers depth in a moment, using the depth *of* a moment. When a poem fits on a mental screen, then a thought can pierce our busyness. Intensity is our luxury now, not the time it took, say, a hundred years ago, to swim the backstroke through a long, long novel. At this technomoment we must plunge, and poetry offers the deep, quick pool.

Yet as strangely contemporary as this art has become, it involves a timeless childhood pleasure: *rereading*. Talisman poems allow us to experience the remnant pleasure of meeting words we love again and again, something that as adult readers we rarely do. In the childish process of rereading poems, we amiably coexist with ambiguity—the experiencing of many feelings and thoughts at the same time—a state that may be the very definition of adulthood. As we approach poems, we use both our adult understanding and our childhood delight in eating the same meal of the same words day after day. In fact, it is inside our childhood demand to *hear it again* that we exercise the grownup pleasure of reading poetry. We discover that knowing a poem isn't the same as knowing any other type of literature. For one thing, you can feel a poem without really understanding it. We reach a comfort level with the meaning we seek and receive—or don't seek and refuse. The poet rarely shines too bright a light on a subject. As readers, we want to enjoy the play of shadows that makes feeling into meaning, yet not be lost in an obscurity that would make poetry a gloomy thing.

Thus there's a whole specialized vocabulary people hurl about when poems are on the examining table. But with a talisman poem, I always say to people I teach, we can avoid autopsy as a way of understanding—though a little knowledge of anatomy helps. As anatomy divides the body into systems—circulatory, nervous, skeletal—a reader can make an anatomy of a poem.

Reading a poem gives you an almost physical experience of a mental activity. While we sit seemingly still in our chairs, a whole muscular, mental, and emotional life is secretly charging. We don't think of apprehending art as sweaty exercise, but the sharp intake of breath that is recognition—the *oh!* of getting it and the long exhalation, the satisfaction of closure, the relief of understanding—are bodily registers of knowledge. Even in a period of inactivity—ill in bed, or just plain lying down—reading poetry gives you a kind of internal massage. Your organs readjust, they rerelate to one another, as you become aware of a new thought or a new feeling or, more likely, of something you, too, have thought and felt all along. As you meet your own experience through someone else's articulation of it, you are refreshed by having a companion in your solitude.

. . . And Friends

For the most part we think of reading poetry as a solitary fact. Surely it is, but since we have to learn how to do it in order to make it our own private pleasure, it is helpful to begin reading poetry in tandem with at least one other person. Even if you are learning from this book how to read a poem, it is an enterprise that we are embarking on together. Because people feel they need assistance when they read a poem, or at least feel a very immediate need to bounce off someone else a reaction to what they've read, this solitary art takes on a quietly communal aspect.

Often simply by sharing knowledge we enrich what we know, just because we have to reformulate it for someone else. About fifteen years ago I began teaching poetry on a one-to-one basis and found it a new part of my professional life. The waves of reading from the talisman stone that I would throw into the pool between me and just one other person circled out into classes, into lectures, into readings, and eventually into the New York City public transportation system. Literally billions of people read the poetry that I helped choose on the buses and subways of cities all over North America. The intense privacy of collecting my talismans has gone beyond communal—it is now very public. And yet the poems retain their private splendor. People do read *to themselves* after all.

This shimmering verge between what is private and what is shared is the basis of a poetry circle. A poetry circle (which is very different from a writing workshop, where people bring in their own poems to be critiqued by one another or by a teacher) occurs when the mutual reading of poetry is at hand. For me, the circle has its beginnings in the side-by-side reading of a poem by two people. For twenty years, my friend the poet Phillis Levin and I have been haunting restaurants and reading poems as we eat. We actually cannot extricate food from thought. Neither can my friend Georgianna Orsini. She invites me to her house in Florida every year just so we can have a few winter nights when we climb into our jammies by six P.M. to read poems out loud while cooking dinner. My friend William Louis-Dreyfus and I have a poetry circle of outrage—very often on the phone. Usually he calls me up fuming about a poem in *The New Yorker* he doesn't understand. "I don't get this sonofabitch," he says, or, "Listen to this!" *Listen to this* is the phrase that forms a poetry circle.

Our evenings together were rare—Barbara Feldon, Peggy Penn, and I were a tough threesome to schedule—so, in between, we found ourselves embarked on secret journeys of enthusiasm. Each of us wanted to unearth poems that would delight the other two, poems they might not have known. When we finally got together to share our surprises, the underlying, unspoken thrill of our evening was that our poems were somehow listening to *us* as we were listening to one another. The depth of our hearing—the depth of acknowledgment—suspended time almost in the way lyric poems themselves seem to stop time. Circles, which have no beginning or end, transform time into holy space, like talismans of experiencing.

In London, Ontario, my book quartet rotates houses so that cooking is an occasion and not a burden. Sometimes the food is even geared to the writer, such as "What Yeats would have eaten." Susan Downe, Ann McColl Lindsay, Thelma Rosner, and I are not always a poetry circle. Sometimes we are a book club. That is when we read novels. But when we are a poetry circle, the genie of interpretation, of listening together and speaking with direct reference to the words in hand, seems released from a bottle none of us knew we were guarding until we are pervaded with the scent of language and find ourselves suddenly more articulate than we were at any other moment in our day. Poetry causes us to speak the words we didn't know we had, to verbalize the connection between feeling and thought we didn't know how to make, but *do*.

Reading is an act, after all; it is *doing*. The study of a poem brings doing and being together. You can take things apart, see what makes them tick, and return them in the glance of an eye, or an aye, or an I. Sometimes I feel we are restoring those wings torn from poems by bullies with low tolerance for ambiguity—the bullies perhaps we ourselves once were. We all have developed a great tolerance for coexisting meanings. Interpretation, the four of us discover again and again, can refashion and restore and reinvent meaning. Four. Four sides. We began as a square, but poetry has rounded our edges, and now our reading—and our friendship—holds us in a circle.

Two summers ago, at the Frost Place—the site of Robert Frost's New Hampshire farm, now regirded for the group of poetry lovers who come there every year—I gave a lecture entitled "How to Start a Poetry Circle." People were hungry to know how these circles worked, and I gave them some detailed ideas, the ones I describe in Chapter 14. Since then, countless small circles of poetry lovers have started, and ones long in existence have been revalidated. I notice we don't say poetry *likers*. It is *love* that we associate with this art. Learning how to read poetry teaches you the steps to love, that most circular feeling.

CHAPTER TWO

The Three Systems
of a Poem

Just because some of the best things in life are dense and mysterious and in need of understanding doesn't mean there aren't simple ways of talking about them. A simple way of talking about a poem is through its three systems: the line, the sentence, and the image.

Poetry is really the fusion of three arts: music, story-telling, and painting. The line displays the poem's music, the sentence displays its thoughts, and the image displays the vision of the poet. When we talk about the body of a poem—its anatomy—the line is like a skeletal system, the sentence is like a circulatory system, and the image is like a central nervous system. That's all.

Any poem? You mean they *all* have bodies like this? In fact, all poems do. Of course there are borderline examples, like prose poems, but even they feel they must distinguish themselves with a compound name. Do really obscure poems, the ones that fracture syntax and work against logical meaning, have the same bodies, too? Of course they do. Following the three systems through any poem, even the most abstract one, lets a kind of simplicity enter understanding. You may discover that you understood what was going on without consciously knowing it, that you apprehended the poem viscerally, if not intellectually. Even though a poem is made with words, it is only one-third a verbal art. It is equally an auditory and a visual art, which we take into our bodies as well as our minds.

THE LINE. Lines make the music of the poem. They function as a skeleton, holding the poem up. Lines contain every aspect of sound, from how words sound alike and different to how they reflect emotion—how such sounds, in fact, are emotions themselves. The line always means rhythm and sometimes means rhyme. Even a free verse poem that doesn't seem to have a regular rhythm or an obvious rhyme scheme still has the baseline bones of music. The line's music gives us our instinctive understanding of a poem, even when we can't articulate it.

THE SENTENCE. Sentences open up the thoughts of the poem. The mainstay of prose, the storyteller's tool, sentences circulate through the lines of poems, often flowing past the lines themselves, pumping their meaning down through the poem, even when the poem is in fragments or has no punctuation to let us know where sentences begin and end. The sentence appeals to our intellectual pleasure, and following a sentence through a poem often enables us to articulate what we've understood.

THE IMAGE. The image is the visual art of the poem. Functioning as a central nervous system, imagery sends the poet's vision, fired into word-pictures, throughout its length, the way the nerves inside a spinal cord send electrical charges to muscles. The body of each poem is wired a bit differently.

If the line is a way a child apprehends, intuitively, and the sentence is the way an adult apprehends, intellectually, then the image functions as a two-way mirror between these states of understanding. It is both instinctive and constructed. When you are at a loss to understand a poem, following the images (which means tracking the nouns) will often bring to you a clarity you can use to make sense of the rest of the poem.

Poetry and Prose, Two Musics

In every language on the earth, the sentence comes in two parts, like the two hemispheres of our brain. Sentences always have, on the one hand, subjects and, on the other hand, predicates, or verbs. Each sentence is a binary system. Even when we don't care about narration, our capacity for language makes stories of what we think, just because of those subjects and verbs.

The sentence is the only tool prose writers have. They take phrases and build them into clauses. They take clauses and build them into sentences. Then they group sentences into paragraphs. Phrases built into clauses, built into sentences, built into paragraphs. That's it for the prose writer's toolbox. (Of course, this is like saying that the colors of the rainbow are it for the artist's palette, but it is a comfort to know that the basic colors of the world fit into a Crayola box, even though we know we can expand subtleties infinitely.)

Now, anyone who loves prose knows that sentences have their own persuasive rhythms. We have memorized our favorites: the opening and closing lines of novels, the tag lines of films. Sentences have their own music, quite apart from the music of the line of a poem.

This means that each poem has **two** musics. One is the main musical system, the rhythm of the line. The other is the music of the sentence. This double music is what gives poetry its richness and depth. Two arts are working on your ear as the sentence *wraps around* the line. Meanwhile, the third art, imagery, flares across the sky of the poem as the two musics play.

CHAPTER THREE

A Comfort Poem

 LET EVENING COME

Let the light of late afternoon
shine through chinks in the barn, moving
up the bales as the sun moves down.

Let the cricket take up chafing
as a woman takes up her needles
and her yarn. Let evening come.

Let dew collect on the hoe abandoned
in long grass. Let the stars appear
and the moon disclose her silver horn.

Let the fox go back to its sandy den.
Let the wind die down. Let the shed
go black inside. Let evening come.

To the bottle in the ditch, to the scoop
in the oats, to air in the lung
let evening come.

Let it come, as it will, and don't
be afraid. God does not leave us
comfortless, so let evening come.

JANE KENYON

(1947–1995)

On a winter day near the solstice, I met Jane Kenyon for tea. Nearly all the lights in New York City were on, and it was only 4:30 in the afternoon. I had hurried through the dusk, late, and stood catching my breath in the doorway of the Upper East Side tea room. There, among cups as pink as the cheeks of the royals on the *Majesty* magazines placed at each table, Jane sat, in a mahogany chair. She'd come in earlier from her home, Eagle Pond, her husband, the poet Donald Hall's, family farm in New Hampshire. Still and composed, she rested there almost as if she were a portrait of herself, the cloud of her dark hair suspended over her hand-knit sweater. Though it was only a few hours past its middle, the day lay in dusk outside the large window she stared through—behind her, the room in a heated glow.

As I heaved off my coat and barged toward her—we'd

never had a face-to-face meeting before, and I was late and a bit nervous—I thought of her poem "Let Evening Come," in which dusk comes to a midsummer day, on almost the opposite side of the calendar. In her poem, the summer evening, long and stately, unfolds its shadows slowly, unlike the dark that dropped down on our winter solstice. In her poem, the end of day is almost statuesque, just like Jane.

The slow comfort of her poem's lyric voice is a tonic I use to settle myself. Whenever I summon the poem up, its pacing seems to slow down my breathing. But *what* inside her words would give the effect of actually regulating the diaphragm? How does the body of language that a poem assembles seem to change the pacing of the human body receiving it? One of the loveliest—and most ancient—of pacemakers is repetition, and when Kenyon repeats *Let* in "Let Evening Come," the pulse of that syllable becomes a New Hampshire mantra. She uses the oldest of ways we have to coax ourselves into relaxation: murmuring the same word again and again to create a chant, a late-twentieth-century litany.

I plopped down on a needlepoint chair and gushed, "How was China?" She answered serenely, "I took your poem 'The Lull' there."

"The Lull." Was there ever a lull in my own life now? I rushed from teaching children in the daytime to teaching a graduate course at night, cramming in my social life like sweaters crushed, last-minute, into a bursting suitcase.

"What did they think of your work, the Chinese?"

"Oh," Jane hesitated, ever truthful, "I couldn't tell, really."

Although this was our first meeting, Jane and I spoke as though we knew each other well. That is because, in a few postcards and brief calls, we had realized that we knew each other's writing very well. I'd read just about everything she had published. I remember one of my teachers at Johns Hopkins, Cynthia Macdonald, saying to our class that nothing would ever be as important to us as the work of our peers, and certainly this was true in my relationship to Jane Kenyon's work.

"How are you doing with the depression poem?" I asked in our strange, literary intimacy. Jane endured lifelong depressions as well as the drugs used to treat them, which she revealed in a poem called "Having It Out With Melancholy." But our talk was about words, not about a bipolar disorder. We settled down into the rhythms of a writing community of two. Editors, publishers, bites of cucumber sandwiches, magazines, nut bread, what we wanted for our art . . . The day sank around us. The ritual of our murmurings and the pouring of tea served as our form of vespers.

If you read "Let Evening Come" aloud, you can feel a vespers resonance. The rhythm of the dozen *Let*s Jane Kenyon uses can lull you into an attitude of prayer. Yet her poem provides the liveliest kind of devotion because the language both repeats *and* quickens with change. Like the mottled light of dusk, the *Lets* move in a scattered pattern, like most patterns in nature.

By the time I reach the end of "Let Evening Come," when she states that God does not leave us comfortless, I completely believe her. But what in Kenyon's plain vocabulary would be responsible for the raptness—and immediacy—of not only my belief but that of most people who read her? Harbored in the poem is the steady pulse of the hymn line, or common measure. It is a loosely constructed hymn, counting often—though not always—eight syllables per line, generally with four beats of emphasis. (*"It* CAME *up*ON *the* MID*night* CLEAR," begins the Christmas carol.) Jane, herself a churchgoer, understood intuitively how music underpins the power of a poem's emotion. We can think of the beat beneath the hymn line as loudness and softness alternating. She puts the loud syllable first: *LET the* CRICK*et* TAKE *up* CHAF*ing.*

If you are in a hurry, your internal rhythm accelerates till all the syllables inside your head are loud. Your mental pulse imitates the loud buzz of fear. Being inside frenetic activity is like being, rhythmically, in the staccato grip of fear. Each syllable of your life seems stressed. By removing half the loudness, by equalizing its emphasis with softness, Kenyon creates a steadiness—or the exact opposite of an adrenaline surge. Fear has a rhythm of overemphasis. By de-emphasizing the fear state, in which your heart pounds in your ears, the poem regulates your in- and exhalations, slowing your breathing.

The stress of overemphasis is partly responsible for what destroys our perspective in life. When we are too consumed by tasks, our mental vista shrinks. Unmitigated emphasis closes the world in on us. De-emphasis actually opens mental space. Quieting sound creates a visual horizon. Kenyon's simple images shine because the musical system has opened up the mental space we need to connect to them. The alternating rhythm clarifies by literally clearing the air, allowing us to breathe with the deep and regular inhalations and exhalations that sustain life.

Our sense of the poem's spirituality comes from this alternating emphasis—or music—moving through each line as its breath. "Spirit," it is nice to remember, *means* breath. Sound, the most subliminal aspect of poetry (though it can be consciously manipulated) carries emotion in a poem in a nearly kinesthetic way. How the poem feels to your tongue and teeth—the consonants, the vowels, the loudness and softness of syllables—is the embodiment of the feelings that sounds evoke. We think poems are about life in language, but they are, as importantly, about nonlanguage, the preverbal experience of emotion, of *being*. One of the reasons we surprise ourselves with our primitive reactions to poetry is that it often recalls us to a preverbal place. Our whole preverbal life, alight with curiosity and interest in everything, occurs *before* we speak recognizable words. The rhythms of lines, as opposed to sentences, can walk the sharpest yet most *unnameable* feelings through the poem. Lines move in ways we are unaware of—just as we move through space without awareness of the momentum of our bones.

While the line is drumming a musical baseline, the sentence, that most conscious of linguistic constructions, is making music, too. In fact, you can see and hear both kinds of music working in "Let Evening Come." The first stanza is a sentence in itself:

> *Let the light of late afternoon*
> *shine through chinks in the barn, moving*
> *up the bales as the sun moves down.*

But the second stanza is two sentences, and so is the third. Though each sentence begins with *Let*, Kenyon places them differently, creating a sentence rhythm with each stanza. And this is what stanzas are all about. Although they sometimes act as paragraphs, and even look like them, they don't always signal or elaborate new ideas the way prose paragraphs do. They are musical groups. *Stanza*, in Italian, means room; you can think of stanzas as musical chambers, as the chambers of a shell. In this poem they are just as pearly and luminous as natural objects because they are both symmetrical *and* asymmetrical. Part of what I think defines beauty in poetry (and this has nothing to do with whether a poet is writing about something pretty or something ugly) is the shimmering verge between what's regularized (in this case, each stanza has three lines, and each sentence, at least in the beginning, starts with *Let*) and what emerges from the regularity—the bump in the shell wall, the mercurial pearl of the color (in this case, the way the sentences move irregularly through the stanzas). The poem's unevenness in spite of its evenness displays a delicious tension between the predictable and the surprising. It is as if someone decided to build a picket fence with varying fenceposts, so that the line of the fence became a wave.

When the title of the poem pops up at the end of the second stanza in its own sentence, it makes you realize that the title itself is a complete thought, with its own subject and verb. The subject is You (understood). Oh my goodness—is the subject God? Or is it Us? Is it *we* who are to relax enough to let evening come? Is it *we* who are to slow our breathing so that things might end with the pace that belongs to them? Oh dear, the whole universe is here, and we are only nine lines down:

> *Let the cricket take up chafing*
> *as a woman takes up her needles*
> *and her yarn. Let evening come.*
>
> *Let dew collect on the hoe abandoned*
> *in long grass. Let the stars appear*
> *and the moon disclose her silver horn.*

The soothing "l" sound that begins the first word of the first line, like an arm slipped around a shoulder, also begins the second and third stanzas, then appears in the middle of the third line of the second stanza and the second line of the third stanza, interrupting the pattern, making it more complex. After that comes the fourth verse, when the poet rubs four *Lets* through the stanza—as if that arm around us were rubbing our shoulders.

> *Let the fox go back to its sandy den.*
> *Let the wind die down. Let the shed*
> *go black inside. Let evening come.*

Now another aspect of rhythm besides regularity comes into the poem. It is pacing. Human beings have subtle responses—and the mechanisms that operate in poetry are subtle, too. Pacing takes that alternating hymn rhythm and colors it with individual response. In the line *Let the FOX go BACK to its SANdy DEN,* the loudness shifts. The hymn line, eight syllables, stretches to ten. The regularity of how syllables alternate soft and loud in common measure also stretches, expanding and contracting in this line, because even though there are two extra syllables there are still the same four beats. Those two extra unstressed syllables, like soft breaths, introduce the fox. After the fox enters the poem, the next line goes right back to eight syllables. Yet because the next two sentences end mid-line, the pacing shifts again. The periods at each midpoint give these two lines a clipped quality. There's a quickening—evening is coming faster.

But it is two tiny, lowercase *let*s in the last two stanzas that trigger the little miracles of this poem. In the fifth stanza *let* seems at first nowhere to be found—then we discover it, protruding its lowercase head.

> *To the bottle in the ditch, to the scoop*
> *in the oats, to air in the lung*
> *let evening come.*

Kenyon's withholding of the *let* until the last line of the stanza internalizes it. It is deep inside its sentence, as air is deep in the lung, or the scoop is deep in the oats. How specific and shiningly individual she makes the bottle by placing it *in the ditch* so familiarly that we are included in her perspective—of course, we know what ditch it is; now we too are part of the everyday evening landscape she inhabits. Lowering the case lowers the poet's voice. Jane herself had a low, calm voice. As the voice of another enters us—slowly, just as the evening comes—our own biology seems to change. Another breath is inside us. When people feel inexplicably changed by—charged by—poetry, part of that inexplicability is this bodily mystery.

It is lovely to remember that the preposition is supposed to have been Gertrude Stein's favorite part of speech. Prepositions are our most private speech parts. They achieve intimacy by showing relations, relationships, and meeting places, sometimes so secret that we forget them. *To the bottle in the ditch, to the scoop/in the oats, to air in the lung:* in two short lines are six prepositions, each showing another slip of relation, another sliver of closeness. As readers of these prepositions, we grow more deeply intimate with the evening—and with the poem itself—becoming more aware of our own biology; finally it is possible to feel ourselves *in* that lung, even as the rhythm of the poem is *in* us. Both the bottle and the scoop are in positions of rest, lying down in their environments, ready for the miracle of restoration that is sleep, or the closure that dissolves the known world and that is death.

There really are only two subjects of lyric poetry, and these are the two things that most rivet our attention: love and death. They are locked by a link of language—*and*—which is an example of my own favorite part of speech, the conjunction. In the presence of the absence that this poem portends grows a mild-mannered, seemingly insignificant word: *so.*

> *Let it come, as it will, and don't*
> *be afraid. God does not leave us*
> *comfortless, so let evening come.*

So is a conjunction; it joins ideas, healing ruptures. As prepositions show us relations, conjunctions make unions. They marry ideas; they are stable and encompassing. And snugly familiar. We almost don't notice them. In the last stanza, before the conjunction slips in, the address of the *Let* changes. *Let it come,* she says in a kind of acceptance tinged with resignation, *as it will.* Then follow the most reassuring words in English, *don't be afraid.* For any work of art to supply an answer—as it is not at all obligated to—is a thing of satisfaction so complete that it sends roots into the soul.

Here is the moment when we realize how much the music of the poem, with its injection of a soft syllable between most louder syllables, has diminished the constant stress of everyday being. The *un*stressed syllables have slowed and calmed the lines. When Kenyon says *don't be afraid,* we are prepared to let go of our fear because we have been abandoning the rhythm of fear through the regularity of our breathing. We can accept the idea that we don't have to be afraid because we have slowed down, reattuned ourselves to the intake and exhalation of our breath and the beating of our hearts.

Then she has the kindness to tell us the reason we are not to be afraid. *God does not leave us/comfortless,* she writes, following the line with a comma, that little curve of a pause, itself like a scoop, before she pronounces the ultimate conjunction, *so. So* unites the twelfth and last repetition of *let* with our perception that yes, darkness *will* fall—and it will be all right now, with all of us, even the darkness of death that is part of the pattern.

. . .

The tea room was empty by the time Jane and I finished our scones with clotted cream and strawberry jam. The little meal was in fact so big that we'd ruined our dinners— Jane didn't know how she was going to manage a big evening meal after the reading Don was about to give. I didn't know then that those few hours would be the first and last time I spoke with Jane face-to-face. There we made a poetry circle in the single instance of a late afternoon, framed by brief letters, a postcard or two, a few phone calls.

Jane Kenyon died of leukemia at age forty-seven, in 1995. In that early-evening-in-the-afternoon of our tête-à-tête, she seemed happy and avid with gossip, not feeling ill at the time, or not expressing it. But all poets will tell you how prescient their poems often are. Dusk was coming, though it was only a few hours past the middle of the day.

When I wake up in the middle of the night, as I often do, "Let Evening Come" is one of the poems I turn to. In the face of my roused anxieties, it reinforces my need to let things shut down, and I find the poem's rhythms deeply restoring. Yet there is always a place in a poem where repetition becomes oppressive, and the poem must seek a change. When I come to the penultimate stanza of "Let Evening Come," I feel how Kenyon quickens the language, growing the poem off the trellis of its pattern. It is like throwing off the weight of too many blankets. She quietly shows that there must be a shift from pattern to conclusion, an opening into what is beyond the scaffolding that repetition makes yet can be discovered only because limits are set: the sudden perspective of grace.

CHAPTER FOUR

A Queen Sends
an SOS

 Wulf and Eadwacer

The men of my tribe would treat him as game:
if he comes to the camp they will kill him outright.

        Our fate is forked.

Wulf is on one island, I on another.
Mine is a fastness: the fens girdle it
and it is defended by the fiercest men.
If he comes to the camp they will kill him for sure.

        Our fate is forked.

It was rainy weather, and I wept by the hearth,
thinking of my Wulf's far wanderings;

one of the captains caught me in his arms.
It gladdened me then; but it grieved me, too.

Wulf, my Wulf, it was wanting you
that made me sick, your seldom coming,
the hollowness at heart; not the hunger I spoke of.

Do you hear, Eadwacer? Our whelp
       Wulf shall take to the wood.
What was never bound is broken easily,
our song together.

ANONYMOUS

(Tenth century)

Translated by Michael Alexander

In some moments of desperation we are thrilled by hope, spurred by a lunatic urge to build a signal fire on our lonely island, lured by the thought of someone, anyone, who might read our message. More than a thousand years ago, the wife of a tribal chieftain, a now-anonymous queen, was driven to send an SOS in verse form. It is the Old English poem we now call "Wulf and Eadwacer" (pronounced Ed-wacker). And it is due to one man only that we hear her passionate voice, the first evidence in English of a poem composed by a woman. Composed is hardly the word for it—she belts out her poem, then she keens. Hers is a thrilling cry—it makes you want to respond to the emergency immediately, even though you'd be centuries late.

If central casting sent us someone to staff the medieval 911 lines, of course we'd be sent a monk. And a monk, also anonymous, is exactly who saved the queen—or at least saved her poem. One day he sat down to copy out his favorite verses—his talismans—making his personal anthology, and among his chosen was what became known as "Wulf and Eadwacer." We call him the Exeter scribe because what he wrote eventually became a gift to Exeter Cathedral from its first bishop, Leofric, who died in 1072. Scholars date the manuscript to sixty or seventy years before Leofric became bishop. If that anonymous scribe had not followed his own affinities, we would not have this poet's voice. Nowhere else, not in one single other book, or box, or pamphlet is this poem recorded. If we believe that acts of charity become great acts only when they are anonymous, then the anonymous rescuing of this rich, clear, anguished voice surely qualifies.

As a university sophomore I was consumed by the Middle Ages, enamored of their spiritual glamour and physical depredation. There, love and death were viscerally intertwined, as I distinctly felt sex and the soul were. Sex was rampant among the barbarians who were gnawing chunks of greasy fowl roasted over the fire in the Great Hall, washing it down with mead in one hand while the other clasped a wench, just as monks in the monastery next door were furiously preserving wisdom with their calligraphy, restored by their herbal remedies after they'd exhausted themselves with Gregorian chants. In Medieval Lit class I was caught in the sexy rasp of the voice of this queen. (Scholars presume from the grammar that she is a woman, though occasionally someone argues otherwise.) The "I" of her voice gave the chasm of time an instant glow of passion—unabashed adultery and motherhood and loss. She cried out the unvarnished truth of her life in a form of English so old I had to depend on a translator to read it.

Ambiguity, if you can live with it, is like a delicious web of clues. The anonymous "Wulf and Eadwacer" poet may not have been a queen; in fact, she may have been the wife of a tribal chieftain, but scholars let us know for sure that she understood the rules of poetry in her day well enough to break them, even as she knew the social rules—savage in her savage time—well enough to break those, disastrously, too.

Medievalist Jane Toswell, professor of English at the University of Western Ontario, informs me that "Wulf" was probably in existence well before the Exeter Book, in an earlier, more oral era. And she reminds me of all the many translations of the poem. Scholars have passed the manuscript along like a love note, and in the traveling through so many hands the sense of some of the original vocabulary has been blurred. For instance, there are words we don't know because they are mentioned only once, and the context is unclear. Translating our own language is like tracing our family tree, a wonder of discovery and frustration.

We barely recognize written Anglo-Saxon (the root of English) as resembling our language, so we cannot read this vigorous and romantic poem without help. Yet in a translation, the translator's voice—and soul—twines about the writer's. It is like a doubling of that aspect of the poem that makes us *its* talisman even as we make it *ours*. A translation takes our own souls, as readers, and intertwines them with the poet. The degree of depth and suddenness of our connection depends on the ease of the translator's ventriloquism.

I have read many other, perhaps more accurate, translations of "Wulf," but Michael Alexander's is my favorite because it gives the flavor of how poems were constructed in Old English while standing on its own as his creation. He seems to climb inside that ancient voice with the very first line, *The men of my tribe would treat him as game.* Immediately he sweeps us into her tribal world of chieftains, the world before the Christian conversion, the world of hunt and game—and the hunted. We know there is a one—a man—who is against the many, hopelessly so: *if he comes to the camp they will kill him outright.* Plunged into a world where little is stable, we hear this voice telling us of the rules, the laws that make things cohere, and that if those laws are broken, the sharpest penalty will be extracted. These first lines always seem cold and damp to me as I try to imagine the weather, the humidity of blood sport, and try to imagine the absence of a roof over my head and what, in lieu of the couch I sit on and the curtains at my window and the books snug in their cases, I would cling to. What, in the world of objects, would she attach to? A few beads? A patch of cloth? A rough enameled pendant like the ones displayed in the British Museum?

To the speakers of our language in its ancient roots, the sounds of the beginnings of words are the most important. To hear those "f"s of *Our fate is forked* is to hear with their ears and to be mesmerized by alliteration, the repetition of these beginning sounds. The front sounds are the teeth and lips of English, and Old English poetry is shaped from word beginnings. We heard the "c" sounds of *come, camp,* and *kill,* but it is in the half line (which Alexander indents) that the "f"s of *fate* and *forked* come to pierce us, for now we know the extremity of the poet's situation: someone to whom this speaker attaches great importance will be killed if he comes to her. To want what is denied to you is the underpinning of most lyric poetry, and the foundation in English of the lyric lament.

This poem in type does not look the way it does in the Exeter book. The scribe wrote it in paragraph form, squashing it between his margins. Here the translator gives the sounds room—hoping to emulate how the poet spoke it. A spoken poem shows us how the tongue makes words—and it's nice to remind ourselves here that "poet," or *scop* in Old English, which is pronounced "shope," means maker. The translator tries to show us how sophisticated medieval alliteration works in the next line, *Wulf **is** on one **island**, **I** on another.* We learn just how separated Wulf and the speaker are through words that begin with vowels. Vowels are the emotional parts of the alphabet that come closest to moans and cries. The speaker's voice is so urgent as it bleeds through the translation that you almost don't notice Alexander's "i"s and "o"s, but they are very much there, and so are the "f"s in the next two lines: *Mine is a **fastness**: the **fens** girdle it/and it is **defended** by the **fiercest** men.*

Most poems we read hug the left margin of a page. A medieval poem acts as if the lines were centered on a page, with an empty trough going down the middle, something like this:

————————————   ————————————

——————————————   ——————————————

————————   ——————————

——————————————   ——————————

In the middle of every Old English line, there is a stop much more pronounced than an ordinary pause and that deep pause is called a *caesura*. The alliteration of a line always relates to that deep pause. The two loudest syllables (the stressed syllables) in the first part of the line begin with the same letter, and one of the two loudest syllables *after* the caesura also alliterates. Alexander makes it easy when he explains that every Anglo-Saxon line has this pattern:

Bang   Bang   Bang   Crack

Here is the *bang, bang // bang, crack* sound in the next line:

If he COMES to the CAMP [deep pause] *they will KILL him for SURE.*

Then the poet adds her own design, the repeated half line, *Our fate is forked*. This repetition, found nowhere else in the poetry of her time, makes her lyric the first lament in English. Professor Toswell tells me that the quirky and refreshing use of repetition is one of the reasons that scholars understand this poem to be whole and not a fragment.

To be literally camped on two islands makes the problem of Wulf and the speaker even worse. Hers *is a fastness;* her camp is there to stay, and she is locked into its customs. The fens (marshy bogs) wrap it tight as a belly is wrapped in a girdle, which makes you wonder about the connection between fen and defense—or fence. Some scholars feel it is Wulf who is imprisoned, that it is his island which is girdled.

Perhaps they are both imprisoned, each on their own island. She tells us excitedly how deep the defense of this island is, and how surely Wulf will die if he approaches, and that their fate will wrench them apart. To evoke what is not present is one of the jobs of the maker, the scop, and this poet wields her repetition wand. Repeated sound, because it *insists* on its presence, can bring the disparate together, even envision the disappeared, creating a union in spirit.

By now we are sure that Wulf must be a lover, torn from his beloved, the speaker, as lovers often are. After all, the poet says, splicing together for all time the connection between inner and outer weather: *It was rainy weather, and I wept by the hearth,/thinking of my Wulf's far wanderings.* Miserable, she opts for substitution: *one of the captains caught me in his arms.* More than a thousand years after she composed her poem, we still seek the advice, the model, of the woman who knows what she needs and seeks to have it, even though, as we all learn from our experiences, the substitute never really replaces the lost love. As she admits: *It gladdened me then; but it grieved me, too.* Her life force bursts from the poem; she is a living female who inverts the juicy Hollywood stereotype of the barbarian and his wench. This wench has *her* barbarian—and she can admit her grief. Scholars don't dispute this part of the poem; the language is stunningly clear.

When grief enters the poem, the sickness of the need unmet, she calls out to Wulf, reminding us that poetry itself has been called "the art of naming." Until now she has been speaking to us, telling us her story. But when she recognizes her pain, she calls directly to him: *Wulf, my Wulf, it was wanting you/that made me sick, your seldom coming,/the hollowness at heart.* We accept without question that Wulf must be a lover, one who seldom comes to receive the passion that this clearly passionate woman can bestow. And it is that *hollowness at heart* that has made her sick, *not the hunger I spoke of* she says in Alexander's phrasing. But what is this hunger? Is it the gift/game hunger for actual food (*treat him as game*) she speaks of earlier in the poem? Is the hunger *not* directly in the poem but only a reference to private conversation with Wulf? The Old English words of the first line quite literally mean "The men would welcome him as a gift." Scholars have associated the word "gift" with food.

Now we, as readers, helplessly overhear another address, for she turns to speak to another man, Eadwacer. Reading these last two stanzas is like overhearing emotional tumult through the wall of the next apartment. Huge figures thunder at each other, beseeching and imploring, but the wall muffles everything they say. Besides, they're not neighbors we know. We may never even have seen them in the hall. Who are they? What is their context? How do we locate them and their feelings? Context is what the scribe of the Exeter Book did not supply us. *Do you hear, Eadwacer?* the poet says, as if to a husband (for it is often husband types who fail to hear). *Our whelp/Wulf shall take to the wood.*

What? Wulf is a *whelp*? A pup? A *child*? Isn't he a lover? Do we have the situation wrong? But maybe whelp can be a term for a young pup, a weaned wolf. . . . Surely the original Old English will tell us. Quick, e-mail Jane Toswell.

The word "whelp," the professor replied, has confused scholars as much as it confuses us. Some say Eadwacer is the poet's husband, a chieftain who has expelled her lover, Wulf, from the camp. Others hold that Wulf is the poet's son. A student of hers is sure that Eadwacer is the forbidden lover, and Wulf the bastard child the poet bore him. The student takes as her proof the phrase of the next line, *What was never bound*. We all turn the story of Wulf toward our own lives and fantasies, listening through the plaster of centuries. Trying to hear the original voice through a translation makes that wall even denser.

When scholars struggle over seemingly insignificant details, they are acting as *our* Exeter scribes, preserving, explaining, reconstructing. Translators of ancient texts are like restorers of paintings, aiming to reveal the original vibrancy of the colors of language. We cannot know the intention of the poet, but we can explore the palette of words she had at her disposal. But nothing in that palette yields a clue about *whelp*.

Could the use of *whelp* mean that motherhood has been the passion that drives the poem? Has what we have interpreted as romance been the adoration of a mother for her son? And who are we to assume that romantic love exists in a culture such as this? One thing we can be certain of is the poet's desperation. The vibrance, the virulence of her distress, comes to us in the calling of those names, Wulf and Eadwacer. Wulf is an unusual name in Old English, Jane Toswell says, in which people were typically called the names of human characteristics, such as "Redbeard," not the names of animals. So this man Wulf is a mysterious stranger merely by the fact of what he is called. But no matter what an individual name signifies, we know for sure that the imploring of a person by name is a distress call. This is an emergency—a tragedy, even.

We hear the tragedy spoken out loud, with an intensity that has never been clouded with question, and experience the clarity of her full, final acknowledgment: *What was never bound is broken easily,/our song together.* But what has not been broken is the poet's attachment to us, the readers of her lament. Through the fine hand of the Exeter scribe, we have her song, we are bound to her song. Her cry upsets us, even over the chasm of time. This is the force of poetry, even in translation—especially in translation, for Alexander is our Exeter scribe, preserving her emergency in the words of his SOS.

Translators are heroes because they try to find ways out of the bind—the fen—of term equivalence: should they be true to the literal words or to the truth they feel lies within them? We are lucky to know the past through the grace of these caretakers, scholars and translators. Perhaps our own times, and perhaps even our voices, will be reinvoked by the cybermonks of the third and fourth millennia. Who knows? They may even find clear meanings for Anglo-Saxon words that escape us now. But we hope our feelings will surge through any words they can't decipher. The communicative energy of poetry, even without all its vocabulary, is what the anonymous poet demonstrates so regally—the power of our fiercest desires.

CHAPTER FIVE

Self-Portraits

 ## WOMEN'S LOCKER ROOM

The splat of bare feet on wet tile
breaks the incredible luck
of my being alone in here.
I snatch a stingy towel
and sidle into the shower. I'm already soaped
by the time a white hand turns the neighboring knob.
I recognize the arm as one that had flashed
for many rapid laps while I dogpaddled at the shallow end.
I dart an appraising glance: She arches down
to wash a lifted heel, and is beautiful.
As she straightens, I look into her eyes.

For an instant I remember human sacrifice:
The female explorer led skyward,

her blonde tresses loose on her neck;
the drums of our pulses grew louder;
I raised the obsidian knife.
Violets bloomed in the clefts of the stairs.

I could freeze her name in an ice cube,
bottle the dirt from her footsteps
with potent graveyard dust.
I could gather the combings from her hairbrush
to burn with her fingernail clippings,
I could feed her Iago powder.
Childhood taunts, branded ears,
a thousand insults swirl through my memory
like headlines in a city vacant lot.

I jump, grimace, divide like an amoeba
into twin rages that stomp around
with their lips stuck out,
then come suddenly face to face.
They see each other and know that they
are mean mamas.
Then I bust out laughing
and let the woman live.

MARILYN NELSON

(b. 1946)

I Am

I am—yet what I am, none cares or knows;
  My friends forsake me like a memory lost:
I am the self-consumer of my woes;
  They rise and vanish in oblivion's host,
Like shadows in love's frenzied stifled throes:
And yet I am, and live—like vapours toss't

Into the nothingness of scorn and noise—
  Into the living sea of waking dreams,
Where there is neither sense of life or joys,
  But the vast shipwreck of my life's esteems;
Even the dearest, that I love the best
Are strange—nay, rather, stranger than the rest.

I long for scenes where man hath never trod
  A place where woman never smiled or wept
There to abide with my Creator, God,
  And sleep as I in childhood sweetly slept,
Untroubling, and untroubled where I lie,
The grass below—above the vaulted sky.

JOHN CLARE
(1793–1864)

Illuminating self-portraits are never vain. The rigor of self-portraiture requires a portraitist to hold her gaze steady in the face of what she fears to see—her puny, her flabby, her ill-gotten being. It requires her to suffer herself, and to be longsuffering is the meaning of the Latin verb *indulgere*. Often we are horrified to be called "self-indulgent," but meaningful self-portraiture requires such honesty and technical skill that it undermines superficial self-absorption. To examine your own *is-ness* without posturing—and with the depth of sympathy you would accord any other subject, even a weed—is both the goal and the process of self-description. With a warm eye for your own human essence, you can reach out in surprising kindness toward the rest of the world.

Self-tolerance—it's your humanity you're suffering, after all—allows a person to be interested in herself with the keenly neutral love of the disinterested portraitist. But to mount this perspective of interior life in a poem takes enormous skill on the part of the poet. She must express herself with consciousness, witnessing her own experience by framing it with a musical system, a system of meaning, and a system of imagery. This permits a poet to indulge a reader with an interior landscape that becomes a model for what we all look like inside. That is just what Marilyn Nelson and John Clare do. On the face of it, it seems bizarre to link a nineteenth-century British white male Romantic poet with a twentieth-century African-American female poet, but lyric poems are like puzzle pieces that fit in myriad placements, not just one. Lyric poetry often prefers interior time and space to historical, locatable moments. Isn't that what we mean when we talk about soul mates? Great self-portraiture creates a soul mate of the reader as well as of poets ordinarily separated by social, political, economic, and racial boundaries.

There *was* a locatable moment when I first met Marilyn Nelson, though. It was in Zion, Illinois, in 1976, at a conference for Danforth Fellows. I felt as though the hand of God in the guise of the Danforth Foundation had scooped me out of my failing young marriage and stumbling "career" as a college administrator and said, "Go study poetry again." "Career" means a course, a road, a way, from the Latin, *carrus*, a wagon. We were rolling out toward the rest of our lives when we met as a group of two in a hotel lounge under a sign that said POETRY.

There I saw her first poems, full of mermaid imagery. Half-fish, half-woman, and half-scholar, half-poet, she was emerging toward what she would be, and she endured what all academics with a creative bent suffer. Would she be a real scholar if she also indulged her creative side? As she gained her footing with her work,, getting her bearings as a woman, too, her poems shed their gills and fins—and stood up. Goodbye, mermaids. I didn't discover all of this immediately. We lost touch for years until we found ourselves on a stage together, reading our poems that had been selected for the *Morrow Anthology of Younger American Poets*. There I heard her recite "Women's Locker Room." The voice of that poem was as big as a world. It established a world, in fact—from the inside out. She'd drawn a self-portrait so bold that I recognized practically everyone I know, including me, inside it, and that's the paradox of self-portraiture: it gives observers insight through details that belong utterly to someone else.

A locker room is an external space where the inhabitants are naked. The idea of a locker room, a place where the accoutrements of the material world, things like wristwatches and money and clothes, are incarcerated, and the body, which is always publicly clothed, now is publicly freed, reverses our ideas of privacy. All reversals present challenges, but locker rooms—jailing the public and releasing the private! Being alone there offers a bodily freedom we rarely experience outside our own bathrooms—and in a solitude far more capacious than those within four close walls. This moment alone is a definition of contentment, a thing to possess, and of course we resent the destruction of our temple of solitude, the cherished place where we were at peace with our fatness, our knobbiness, the physical manifestation of our hairy souls.

> *The splat of bare feet on wet tile*
> *breaks the incredible luck*
> *of my being alone in here.*
> *I snatch a stingy towel*
> *and sidle into the shower.*

Of course the speaker grabs that *stingy towel*—why are they always so skimpy?—and to preserve that fleeting sense of privacy, she *sidles*, like the thief of her own solitude, into the sanctum sanctorum, the shower. If a locker room were a place of worship, the shower would hold the holy tablets.

> *I'm already soaped*
> *by the time a white hand turns the neighboring knob.*
> *I recognize the arm as one that had flashed*
> *For many rapid laps while I dogpaddled at the shallow end.*

The poet has a moment to soap herself until the appearance of that *hand*, belonging to the fast-lane racerbacked cowgirl who has carelessly—probably unknowingly—bested her in the pool. To add insult to injury, the intruder is not only a superior athlete, but gorgeous, and Caucasian.

> *I dart an appraising glance: She arches down*
> *to wash a lifted heel, and is beautiful.*
> *As she straightens, I look into her eyes.*

The intruder's privacy, too, has been dislodged. At this edge of reality, between public and private space, between exterior and interior life, identity is defined.

> *For an instant I remember human sacrifice:*
> *The female explorer led skyward,*

her blonde tresses loose on her neck;
the drums of our pulses grew louder;
I raised the obsidian knife.

Marilyn Nelson is possessed of a murderous thought—
and risks admitting it to us, her readers. That is the gamble
of intimacy some poets make. But Nelson's voice isn't confidential, it's mythic. Her urge to kill is a stately idea: *For an*
instant I remember human sacrifice. The earliest poems, some
people believe, accompanied sacrifice and its religious ritu-
als. Nelson conjures up a Hollywood image: a white stereotype of deepest, darkest Hollywood Africa, where the
natives are restless, beating their drums like the speaker's
pulse. The imagery is B movie, but the vocabulary is not; *the*
obsidian knife is more like an elegant artifact. The unsus-
pecting female intruder/explorer is now a captured colo-
nialist invader being led to her death. Yet in another way,
the poet herself is a female explorer.

Along with this new question of identity, up springs a
strange, unrelated line, *Violets bloomed in the clefts of the*
stairs. In this line the three systems of the poem suddenly
overlap: a full sentence fills a full line with a fully formed
brand-new image. Because of the word "clefts," I have an
image of female genitals, the clitoris and labia like violets in
the cleft of the outer lips. I suppose those stairs are where
the white explorer is led up to her sacrifice, but what are
those violets doing there—suggesting by image such soft-

ness, but by sound a contradictory *violence?* Even as the speaker of the poem wants to murder the other woman, she seems to merge with her.

Identity is no simple matter, as a quick student in one of my classes at the Poetry Center of the 92nd Street Y in New York confirmed. She remembered a passage from the *Song of Solomon*, 2:14, which mentions both clefts and stairs. The King James version reads, "Oh my dove, that art in the clefts of the rock, in the secret places of the stairs, let me see thy countenance." Here those very images are used in a game of lovers' hide-and-seek. As lovers desire to gaze at the beloved, so enemies want to meet face-to-face. After all, both types of couples are intimately bound in their relationships.

Now the evil intent takes a voodoo route—still in keeping with the earliest uses of poetry, spells, and amulets as wards against curses. The poet goes one better than sticking pins into a doll—she invents her own magic spell, freezing the woman's name. (Because poets are namers, stopping the power of a person's name means the opposite of poetry.) But Nelson miniaturizes the threat. The name is frozen not in an ice*berg* but in an ice *cube*. She takes her readers from the equator to the fridge. As this poem plays with intimacy and distance, size and proportion, it plays with race. After all, it's a *white* hand and *blonde* tresses the poet is going to practice her voodoo on. Not only is it jealousy that she portrays, it's vengeance, bottling that dirt, burning those fingernail clippings. Nelson's system of the image creates a tinderbox of nouns: *ice cube, dirt, graveyard dust, combings, clippings, powder.* Then her system of the sentence ignites them with these verbs: *freeze, bottle, gather, burn,* and *feed.* In this miniature conflagration, pieces of identity also go up in smoke. The speaker, a literary woman who steeps her poem in references, now identifies with a Shakespearean character, the conniving white Iago, who tricks the black king Othello into distrusting his Desdemona. The ashes of their identities mix, reminding me that the Indo-European root of black and of white (*blanche*) is one and the same: the word that means ashes, *bhel.*

> *I could freeze her name in an ice cube,*
> *bottle the dirt from her footsteps*
> *with potent graveyard dust.*
> *I could gather the combings from her hairbrush*
> *to burn with her fingernail clippings,*
> *I could feed her Iago powder.*

The whimsical sass of the poet's voice makes spirals, like a kite dipping into the crosscurrents of all the social forces that form an identity in a place and a time. All the insults of her childhood, the poet thinks, could be marshaled against this woman. Those *branded ears*, Marilyn told me via e-mail, were "burned by a hot comb in the process of hair-straightening."

Childhood taunts, branded ears,
a thousand insults swirl through my memory
like headlines in a city vacant lot.

In defining the intruder, Marilyn Nelson defines herself. But the poet's way of definition is through simile, a comparison that uses the word "like":

I jump, grimace, divide **like** *an amoeba*
into twin rages that stomp around
with their lips stuck out,
then come suddenly face to face.
They see each other and know that they
are mean mamas.

She transforms herself into a single-celled animal, the basic unit of her self. Like a she-devil, like a whirling shaman dancer, she jumps and makes faces, then divides. That verb *divide* internalizes the naked two-woman stand-off in the shower. Now the speaker herself is split into *twin rages that stomp around/with their lips stuck out*. What *are* these two rages? The fury against what everybody else values—the athletic blonde sylph—and the fury against herself for buying into it, both overlaid with the fear of her childhood's *thousand insults* and *taunts*. In the release of letting the self divide and dance, the two parts of herself literally see each other.

Often when we say "I see," we mean "I know." To be face-to-face is to confront—and to be honest. Face-to-face means inescapable. In fact, the verb *know* itself jumps up and grimaces in the fourth-to-last line. Each woman is so powerful inside the poet that she recognizes they are in a standoff. Each is a *mean mama*. The fact that they coexist in her recognizably makes her powerful. She owns herself by owning the contradiction that makes her who she is. Then she does what we do when we suddenly get perspective: she laughs. One of the reasons I love this poem is that Nelson—a very serious person—laughs at the end of it. And it's a big laugh, it *bust[s]* out.

> *Then I bust out laughing*
> *and let the woman live.*

What a relief—the anger, understood, bursts forth in laughter and self-affirmation. She holds the power of life and death over the intruder on her privacy, the rival she exorcizes by incorporating. With the intruder safely internalized, Nelson can now literally laugh that woman out again, heaving her into the air from the poet's own diaphragm.

This is a free verse poem, which means that the system of the line is relaxed and irregular. Free verse, where there is no rigid count underpinning the music of each line, is exactly the system of personal music that corresponds to a poem about emerging identity. The body of the poem is made from a stack of thirteen simple declarative sentences, nine of which have the subject "I." The syntax itself is an act of self-definition. By the time Nelson is *soaped*, we've slid into the protection of her "I" and see through her eyes. Is that why "identify" begins with the letter "i"?

Born in England, a century and a half before Marilyn Nelson, John Clare also wrote a poem dominated by a personal pronoun, "I Am." Unlike Nelson, who grew from a tentative writer into a poet who managed to meld her academic and artistic selves, John Clare grew more fragmented with time. In fact, "I Am" was written at Northampton County Asylum, where Clare was confined for the final twenty-two years of his life. The fact that we even have "I Am" at all is due to the house steward of that asylum, W. F. Knight, who, like the medieval scribe who preserved "Wulf and Eadwacer," copied out Clare's poetry and saved it.

Unlike his contemporaries, the British Romantic poets Keats, Shelley, Wordsworth, and Byron, Clare was a poor farm laborer whose mother struggled to keep him in school a few months a year, at least until he was thirteen and had to go to work. The poet Carolyn Kizer tells us in her introduction to her selection of his poems, *The Essential Clare*, that despite his meager education, he managed not only to read but to read widely and well, from the Elizabethan poets through his contemporaries, and to write extraordinary poems. He loved Alexander Pope and another poet who was out of favor in his time—John Donne. By Clare's early teens, Kizer tells us, he was writing ballads and showing them to his parents, who belittled them until he garnered his parents' respect by claiming he'd copied his poems from a book. Clare had many jobs, among them bartender at the Blue Bell pub, and many hours of farm work, and an intense family life—he, his wife, and their seven children lived with his parents in a tiny cottage. But his chief occupation was walking in the countryside, where he observed birds and wrote poems about their habits and their nests.

Miraculously, Clare managed to compile a book of poems called *Poems Descriptive of Rural Life and Scenery*, which was published when he was only twenty-seven. The first year, Kizer says, it sold four thousand copies. (Most North American first books of poetry sell less than a quarter of that.) Of course Clare had to travel to London, where the book was launched. And he suffered in the way every author does—what in hell was he going to wear? He wore what he had, of course, his country clothes. He went to the fancy gatherings in his bright green farmer's coat. He shook hands with Coleridge and de Quincey in his bright green coat. He ate London delicacies in his bright green coat. The bumpkin who sold eight times as well as Shelley was an easy mark in this coat. Critics called him "the green man."

He probably looked like he stepped off a package of frozen vegetables. But all book tours come to their ends, and Clare was soon back home. He needed to support not only his wife and children but also his parents. Clare suffered from bouts of fen ague—the name of a type of malaria, which curiously echoes the fens in "Wulf and Eadwacer." These episodes began to break his physical health; more devastating were his mental breakdowns.

Who knows how Clare would have made out if someone had offered him a Danforth fellowship? But while Shelley romped through Europe and Wordsworth paced at home, the green man Clare was put away. (The local asylum, according to Kizer, wasn't the snake pit we might imagine. The poet actually had some outpatient privileges, thanks to his saving relationship with the warden.) Most poets tap into extremes of emotion; it comes with the territory. Most poets also are tapped by the emotions generated by their time and place—and from which, paradoxically, they produce timelessness and placelessness, as did Clare. "I Am" may have been written in an institution, but that place itself figures nowhere. The literal trade-off for residence in the asylum was that Clare was well fed and physically healthy—and he wrote. People debate the quality of his late poems, but no one doubts the power of "I Am." It is the self-assessment of a lonesome but wise man. Clare must have suffered terribly from his seclusion, but he also must have suffered from the close quarters of his family. "I Am" defines itself by a longing for identity-affirming solitude: *I am—yet what I am, none cares or knows*. The insistence that we *are*, that we exist and therefore have a right to our existence, is so basic to our idea of living that it almost doesn't need to be articulated—except by someone whose existence is challenged daily, perhaps hourly, by his state of mind.

In a richly obvious alternating rhyme scheme (far from Marilyn Nelson's free verse), Clare explores the reality of his state:

> *My friends forsake me like a memory lost:*
> *I am the self-consumer of my woes;*

To be forsaken, lost, in effect to be erased—Clare's identity is challenged by the kind of oblivion the absence of free human contact imposes. He describes those woes as they *rise and vanish* like shadows in *frenzied stifled throes* then reasserts, *And yet I am, and live*. If "Women's Locker Room" can be about what's constrained—what's imprisoned between women and in the self—then "I Am" is about what can never be suppressed, in spite of all the ways society and the self conspire to jail it: the essence of who a person is, his *sawol*.

With the calmness of a pianist who is able to bring each finger down with the same weight on each key, Clare stresses every other syllable equally in the first line, a loud

iambic pentameter that stresses the *am* in *I am*, emphasizing the power of that state-of-being verb. An iamb is the
lub DUB, lub DUB rhythm of a heartbeat. Iambic pentameter means there are five iambs: *I AM yet WHAT I AM,
none CARES or KNOWS.* In the second line, however, the
stresses take on different weights or colors: *My FRIENDS
forSAKE me LIKE a MEmory LOST. Like* is almost unstressed, it is so lightly spoken, and *lost* is deeply stressed.
But the lub DUB, lub DUB of a heartbeat pulses with
healthy regularity throughout the lines. No matter what,
even as he is the *self-consumer* of his woes, Clare's beat goes
on. Working the system of the image like a painter who,
with care and accuracy, applies acne scars to the face of his
subject, Clare indulges in a description of these woes. His
avid awareness recalls the late self-portraits of Rembrandt,
in which the aged artist's flesh, so accurately and forgiv-
ingly rendered, looks as if it might feel warm to the touch.
Clare's troubles

> *rise and vanish in oblivion's host,*
> *Like shadows in love's frenzied stifled throes:*

To be both frenzied and stifled—*that* is a definition of
discomfort. The speaker lives

> *like vapours toss't*

> *Into the nothingness of scorn and noise.*

When a sentence winds around lines, the system of meaning merges with the rhythmical system of the poem, and when this sentence then bridges the gap between stanzas, its syntax has a special plasticity. A single sentence extends from the first line through the first two stanzas, sustained by the elegant use of semicolons and dashes through twelve whole lines. Into the *nothingness of scorn and noise*—the strange insubstantiality of the matters that cause us distress—which is also part of

> *the living sea of waking dreams*
> *Where there is neither sense of life or joys,*

the ship of the self plunges. The poet underpaints a vast, pulsing horizon of waking dreams, and in this state of moving, planktonlike neutrality, the ship of *my life's esteems* comes to the disaster of its *vast shipwreck*, where the world inverts.

How many of us, when our world is belly-up, have stared at our families and thought, "They are complete strangers!"

> *Even the dearest, that I love the best*
> *Are strange—nay, rather, stranger than the rest.*

Whimsically, Clare plays on "stranger" with *nay, rather, stranger than the rest*. Part of the sanity of this poem lies in its vigorously playful nature, always taking time to ensure the delivery of its puns and simple rhymes like *best* and *rest*. If artistically you can deliver, then a kind of deliverance is at hand just in the intensity of your making.

The quest for solitude, which in this self-portrait parallels—or perhaps actually *is*—the quest for identity, blooms in the last stanza:

> *I long for scenes where man hath never trod*
> *A place where woman never smiled or wept*

Clare longs for the moment that Marilyn Nelson cherishes. *Solus*, the Latin root of solitude, means alone, single, or one only. I think again of Clare's cramped cottage and of his wife, Patty Turner (whom he married when she was seven months pregnant, Carolyn Kizer tells us, after he became estranged from his childhood love, Mary Joyce, the daughter of a farmer too prosperous for the Clare clan). Both poets connect solitude with the full flush of identity. To be alone is to recognize an individuality that can be lost in the manyness of too much company. We live in a crowded world, a noisome, clamoring place, where our attention is constantly diverted from our stream of being. I know people who do nothing but *respond* all day. They are so tuned to respond that their ability to follow their own course is drained of intention. Clare makes me think again of that reduced vitality. Marilyn Nelson burst from the tightness of her early work—as she busted out laughing—having found the expressive life that Clare searched in vain for. Oneness, the fully integrated essence of who we are, gathered and fully alive—isn't this the state most of us long for? To know who we are is to know why we are living *and*, even better, allows us to extend our energies out into the world.

The cellular contentment of self-knowledge allows a connection to the universe. *Uni-* means one, too, and *-verse* comes from the Latin, meaning, as in plowing a field, to make a row, or line, and the line of course is the crucial element in poetry. Our word for evenly stressed, metrical poetry is "verse." To think of the universe as the one poem that holds us all . . . brings us back to the shimmering verge between loneliness and solitude. Clare might define loneliness as going solo in the universe, without connection; but solitude, he says, means to be alone *within* the universe, *at one* with the grass below and *the vaulted sky* above, *connected*.

> *There to abide with my Creator, God,*
> *And sleep as I in childhood sweetly slept,*
> *Untroubling, and untroubled where I lie,*
> *The grass below—above the vaulted sky.*

The depth of this connection is musical. The last two lines, which have the same end sounds, are a rhyming couplet. The couplet, like a perfect brass hinge, attaches two experiences, *lie* and *sky*, as do *best* and *rest* in the second stanza.

(The rhyme scheme isn't the same in all three stanzas; it's fluid, moving with the emotion and thought of the poem—there aren't any rhyming couplets in the introductory stanza. Clare isn't drawing any conclusions there; he's just beginning.) The closing rhyming couplet is a satisfying sound experience because the rhyme is as complete as the snug closing of a door we want to shut on the world—to ensure our privacy. One rhyme hears its echo; we need echoes to confirm who we are in the world. The echo turns the anxiety of loneliness into the contentment of solitude.

Clare's last image, of the child sleeping, reminds me of the Child Pose in yoga—a pose of rest, "untroubled" and therefore no trouble to anyone, the child sweetly positioned between earth and sky, security below and freedom above. To sleep without interruption (think of the noise of Clare's household, and the noise of the asylum so often preventing sleep) is also to be at one, to find the God within.

We might call the Creator that moving force of creativity within ourselves, what allows us to be the makers, the *scops*, of our lives. To read a poem about oneness as it is revealed in the specifics of genuine human emotion—Nelson's anger and Clare's longing and insistence, neither of these poets wise as Buddha, but exerting their all-too-human energies on existence—is to reach a kind of unity in ourselves, to attend to our own identities. That childlike state that the Romantics knew so much about, the place of innocence that in adults we can call intuition, makes this attention possible, desirable, and maybe even achievable in the presence of poetry, if only because in poems such a state is *mentionable.* Since these self-portraits focus on the details of existence that produce the special conditions in which the poets' *sawols* might thrive, to read them together is both to experience solitude and to connect, through language, to our responsive sameness. And this is what universality means.

CHAPTER SIX

Melancholy Deluxe

 ## No Worst,
There Is None

No worst, there is none. Pitched past pitch of grief,
More pangs will, schooled at forepangs, wilder wring.
Comforter, where, where is your comforting?
Mary, mother of us, where is your relief?
My cries heave, herds-long; huddle in a main, a chief-
Woe, wórld-sorrow; on an áge-old ánvil wince and sing —
Then lull, then leave off. Fury had shrieked "No ling-
ering! Let me be fell: force I must be brief."
O the mind, mind has mountains; cliffs of fall
Frightful, sheer, no-man-fathomed. Hold them cheap
May who ne'er hung there. Nor does long our small

Durance deal with that steep or deep. Here! creep,
Wretch, under a comfort serves in a whirlwind: all
Life death does end and each day dies with sleep.

GERARD MANLEY HOPKINS

(1844–1889)

When we are truly sad, when we are deeply grieved, language lets us acknowledge—and value—that state. We don't live in a culture that lets us grieve to the degree and frequency we need to.

Let a mere week lapse after a divorce and someone is slipping a dating-service number in your pocket. Three days after you have finished the numbing job of cleaning out your mother's house after her funeral, someone will be truly perplexed as to why you don't want to get dressed and go to a party. Unwilling to see you sad, however legitimately, a well-meaning friend may even suggest antidepressants. It seems we can't stand to see our friends, or our mates, or even our acquaintances in the throes of anything but the sunnier emotions—but does happiness actually *have* throes? Not like the bleaker emotions do. One look at the calendar tells you that winter is three months long—a whole quarter of the year. We all have our periodic winters. We're supposed to. They may not fall on a yearly schedule, but occur they do, and we have to give our misery its due.

Probably lots of adults around my miserable fourteen-year-old student Gil thought he should have been on anti-depressants. Gil's poems were full of his tortures: his parents' harangues, his grandfather's illness, his resentment of his younger brother, his own constant low-grade colds and flus that kept him out of school and always behind with his schoolwork, not helped by his daydreaming. His poems were full of the slightly-darker-than ordinary stuff of urban adolescence, except that the art he had attempted made it *his* adolescence, somehow brightly specific because it was *written down*, and not only jammed in a diary, but worked on, developed, worried over as music, imagery, vocabulary itself. The poems were the place where Gil went way beyond wallowing in his misery. They were where he gloried in gloom. There *is* a kind of glory in gloom. Pure distress is a variety of abundance, too.

Loss is a state we all necessarily enter, if only in our dreams. We all lose things, if not people, and time, and . . . *our way*. Yet we are supposed to remedy these losses immediately, get over them, get on with life, and even remove that preposition "with," and simply *get* a life. But life takes time to be gotten. And time and substance are what we will not allow our negativity. No one ever tells you to "get past" falling in love. But falling in loss requires time, too.

All of Gil's feelings felt tangible to him. Yet adults and many kids felt he should "shake them," as if he were a dog coming in from the rain. The fact is he *recognized* his misery because he created language for it and applied language to it, like a bandage.

But do not think that I am telling you poetry is verbal Prozac. And do not think that I am saying Gil grew up into a sexy, smart twenty-five-year-old man with a graduate degree and a fabulous fiancée because he undertook, at age fourteen, a course of self-administered poetry therapy. He simply took a serious interest in poetry. He gave language to how he felt and what he thought, and then he concentrated on that language, changing it, editing it—revising it. Revising means to re-envision, even to revisualize a subject in order to see it better, and then put more precise language to it. Gil was making art. The enterprise of making is not the same as healing, but it lays a foundation for health, if only because mental health requires clarity. Gil was not happy—but he was clear. Part of that clarity came from a recognition of who and what he had to deal with in his life. He really was beleaguered by his parents and brother and grandfather and health and teachers and friends. The urgencies of his writing fleshed out the necessary downbeats. Legitimizing the blue-violet spectrum of personal life is a task that syntax can perform, especially syntax under pressure.

No poet cooks words under more pounds of pressure than Gerard Manley Hopkins. I wish I had thought of sending Gil off to read Hopkins' poem "No Worst." Then without a doubt he would have felt listened to, because he would have overheard a grown man cry. Hopkins was a nineteenth-century British Jesuit priest who was an overworked perfectionist all his life, and initially was so conflicted about poetry and religion that he destroyed all his poetry before taking orders. Later he realized that the muse was a necessary constituent of the way of life that had called him. Gil would have deeply understood the cave shadows of emotions as they surfaced into Hopkins' language. *No worst, there is none* begins the first line of one of Hopkins' Sonnets of Desolation, written in the most despairing part of his life. He had been sent to Dublin as a professor of Greek and Latin literature. There he was responsible for examining hundreds of students. Scrupulously conscientious, agonizing over half- and quarter-points of grades in cold buildings with bad plumbing, donating his salary to the school and in failing health, Hopkins was near a breaking point. But creative clarity about misery brings energy to the life that is, at one moment, not worth living. In fact, creative energy makes living through misery possible, as any survivor knows.

There is a fascinating linguistic side to this. The English sentence has a habit of constructing positively. In fact, to create negativity in English we have *to invert* positive statements. The "n" words, "no," "not," and "never" create a ghost of the positive in every negative. For example, what image does "no plums" conjure up? First, plums perch on an imaginary plane; then you remember they aren't supposed to be there, so you dissolve them. The word "no" gave us the plums, then immediately took them away. Yet they remain in a ghostly outline. The language of "no" mourns what it once had.

When Gerard Manley Hopkins plunges into grief in his sonnet "No Worst," the system of the sentence makes a depth charge of nothingness: *No worst, there is none.* Hopkins garrotes the syntax so there is no doubt of the fathomlessness of the bleakness. He achieves this with both pure negation *and* a ghost negative. He makes a pure negative when he puts *worst* into the position of the subject of the sentence, *worst | is.* Then he makes the *worst* worse by placing *none* into a backup position: *Worst |is| none.*

No, the first word of the poem, its greatest punch, is the muscular adjective of refusal. But since the subject is *worst*, *No* makes a ghost of *worst*, so that *worst* stalks the poem accompanied by its own fierce shadow. And as they patrol the line, they meet themselves again in the predicate as *none. No, worst,* and *none* become the three horsemen of despair.

Hopkins loved the complexity of many layers of address, and loved his own deeply personal rhythms. He went to great lengths to explain his concept of sprung rhythm (Hopkins' term for all the unusually stressed syllables in his work) in essays and in letters to his friend the poet Robert Bridges. To me, Hopkins seems instinctively to understand the Anglo-Saxon origins of English. He incorporates the alliteration of the time of the "Wulf and Eadwacer" poet into his own nineteenth-century line, combining its emphasis on beginning sounds with rhyme's emphasis on ending sounds. The way Hopkins uses the systems of the sentence and the line ties us up and ties us down with word similarities—and creates the glory of gloom.

Hopkins closes the first line with *Pitched past pitch of grief,* spewing those "p"s after the caesura, or midpoint of the line. But his love of first *and* last sounds lets him echo the last two letters of *past* with the last two letters of *worst.* As readers, we are tossed into a maelstrom of syllables, land-ing with a thud on grief, seized by loss, as if nothingness had hands.

Hopkins' poem, a sonnet, actually does seem to have hands. All English sonnets—poems usually of fourteen lines, usually of ten syllables and five stresses per line—have two hands to lend a reader. The opening hand of the octet, or first eight lines, sets you in a mode of thinking about some-thing and the concluding hand of the sestet, or last six lines, turns or resolves the thinking begun in the octet. Some-times the first hand is more active—it could hold you in one idea right down through twelve lines—leaving the other hand for the conclusion. Occasionally you are moved from hand to hand several times. But always somewhere in the last six lines of a sonnet there is a shift in emphasis or point of view. That shift is called a "turn."

What I love about sonnets is the intensity and surprise after this turn. When I write them, I start out thinking that I am going down a lane I know very well—only to discover I've gone across the world. The compression of sonnets has partly to do with a time limit—you have only fourteen lines to say whatever it is—that is, if you *know* what you want to say. Sonnets allow you to discover something rapidly, also because of their compression. They are thrilling to write. I think of them like competitive ice skating—performing a timed routine with compulsory choreographic elements (except no one has taught you the moves).

We know by the second line of the sonnet that Hopkins understands pain, because he can predict its arrival and time its spasms. He tells us confidently that the grief will get worse, saying, *More pangs will, schooled at forepangs, wilder wring.* In Hopkins' poetry it's as if the system of the line grapples with the thrashing limbs of the sentences, trying to hold them, attempting to calm them down. If you were to type this sonnet as a paragraph, it would be far too dense to read. The sentences need the steady beat of the line to open up the emotional pulse behind their meaning, to let the meaning breathe. To do this, Hopkins brings all kinds of sound devices into play. Not only does he use Anglo-Saxon alliteration—*will, wilder, wring*—but he creates assonance (or vowel alliteration) with all the *i*-vowels that follow. Through the sounds of his vocabulary, he excites us to understanding. Instead of veering away from what galls him, and therefore failing to understand it, he speaks his way through agony, twisting his vocabulary into syntactic knots like inflamed muscles. When he interrupts the second line with the phrase *schooled at forepangs* (*forepangs* is a noun wired together from "before" and "pain"), he gives us linguistic biofeedback, showing us how to meet bitter burdens with words.

When Hopkins calls out for rescue—who would not?—saying, *Comforter, where, where is your comforting?/Mary, mother of us, where is your relief?* the fact that he hears no answer leaves him orphaned, in a motherless state. The alliteration eases off when he asks his questions in lines three and four. And with the lessening of alliteration, we start to hear the rhymes at the ends of lines. If you read the end words of the first eight lines down the poem, you will realize that only two sounds move back and forth, words that rhyme with "grief" and "wring." And there are only two sounds that end the next six lines: words that rhyme with "fall" and "cheap." Wisely, Hopkins uses only four sounds to keep pace in the poem because he is wrenching his other vocabulary so hard our tongues feel like crowbars.

> *My cries heave, herds-long; huddle in a main, a chief-*
> *Woe, world-sorrow; on an age-old anvil wince and sing—*
> *Then lull, then leave off.*

He heaves with his sobs, making them visible through the system of the image. His cries are as long as an animal herd, thundering across a plain, their sounds the clang of the forge, the dark forge of feeling, where suddenly, the tongue-clot breaks up and sings as the anvil crashes and the "l"s arrive, *lull, then leave off.*

In Old English poetry, nouns are combined to make new concepts like *herds-long, world-sorrow* or *chief-woe*. (Usually *main* is taken as an adjective that modifies *chief-woe*, for a sense of absolute, or *main*, sorrow. *Main*'s Old English root is *maegen*, or strength. But that word also has the shadow of the ocean or sea heaving, as in waves of sobbing, the bounding main of emotions. This is, after all, a poem about a man crying.)

Astonishingly, Hopkins' clot of grief begins to break up with the breaking up of a word, *ling-ering*. So often, the impulse inside us that makes or creates is subtly at work inside our nether emotions. The urge to create coils inside the urge to destroy. Just at the midpoint of the poem we witness a refreshingly buoyant piece of wordplay that creates as it destroys. At the sound of Fury's screams, almost as if it is called up by Fury, Hopkins' playful creativity bursts through in the form of a hyphen.

Fury had shrieked "No ling-
ering! . . . "

No matter how bad you feel, to break lingering in two is fun. *Ling-ering!* means a life force is at work; the break also causes you to linger—the poet is buoyantly imaginative in his rage. If you view the poem as a body, this midpoint is its stomach and diaphragm—its gut. Just as many of us finally integrate who we are when we speak from the gut, so the playful impulse, the whimsy of the creator, emerges as a rescuing strength.

For at the moment that Hopkins' saving imagination is busy hammering syllables apart (or destroying), it is also rushing to incorporate music into meaning (thus creating), and the pronoun *I* enters the poem. Hopkins steps forth, speaking from the gut: *Let me be fell, force I must be brief.* (*Fell* means fierce—brutally fierce; and the word *force* is shortened from "perforce," meaning by necessity). He asks permission to tell us ruthlessly just what it's like inside his head.

> *O the mind, mind has mountains: cliffs of fall*
> *Frightful, sheer, no-man-fathomed.*

The O begins the turn of the sonnet. Here his identity emerges from his cries. Through the hollow of this capital letter O rush the winds of all emotions. It, too, is negativity embodied. What fills the O? Nothing. Yet the nothing is surrounded, bordered by the black circle of the letter, defined, identified.

Now we are inside the bitter mental landscape where depths roil below the sheer cliffs of consciousness. The falling sensation, the helpless drop down, down, into an abyss that we ourselves contain—who has not felt that abyss open up below, and who has not tried to hold on for dear life? And if you haven't, Hopkins dares you to belittle this state, this full-blown depression, you, who have never been there.

> *Hold them cheap*
> *May who ne'er hung there.*

Then a sickeningly sadistic voice inside his depression speaks, *Here! creep/Wretch.* It is the belittling voice that tells him he is nothing. I can hear the language of the Eucharist, the sinner who is not fit to pick up the crumbs beneath the Lord's table. The wretch is negativity embodied, a zero. How close O and zero are. . . . Yet O means recognition, while zero means absence.

Finally, in the coldest moment of the poem, Hopkins throws himself a blanket.

> *under a comfort serves in a whirlwind: all*
> *Life death does end and each day dies with sleep.*

To *creep . . . under a comfort* seems very much like pulling the covers over your head and simply blanking out, and that's what the poet does.

He never pretends that things are "all right"; he is bleakly truthful. Yes, life does end. And when we face this fact, it is often so enervating that we have to lie down. Hopkins won't find an easy exit from his desolation, but there is a sparing, a comforting, a genuine softening of the terrifying hardness of life evident in the play of the three systems of the poem: line, sentence, and image. The lines of the poem display such a vitality that they undercut—and soften, and brighten, and energize—the harshness of the negativity of the sentences. Music is the positive from which the negative of meaning is made. The poem is alive—and well. It thrives in spite of the speaker. There is an unmistakable vigor to the language of this poem, the exact opposite of waning and death.

Instead of being a poem of suicide, this is a poem of continuing, inside furious bleakness. It is *too alive* with negativity to fall headlong into zero. The quickening of the poem is its wordplay. That essential play with words creates a poet's identity—and rescues us as readers. The rescuing life force of wordplay allows us to be alive within grief and to contain sadness as necessary to who we are. To look a bleak feeling in the eye and feel it, without masking it, is the task that Hopkins sets himself, and that's why I should have given his poetry to a fourteen-year-old boy. I hope Gil found Hopkins by himself.

While it is strange to think of "No Worst" as a safe harbor, it does harbor us from having to flatten out losses we know are rich, real, and all too human. Though the end of Hopkins' poem is horrifying, the vigor of the poem is electrifying. It makes you aware that the underside of daily cheer has its terrifying purple beauty. It asks you to appreciate that the texture of life exists in its nubs, slubs, cliffs of fall, and whirlwinds. When you face the certainty that things won't turn out for the good, here is a poem that not only won't lie to you, but will stick with you as you ride out the worst. Like a homeopathic medicine made from a tincture of poison that in sufficient quantity would kill, but in drops effects a mighty cure, Hopkins' poem remedies our whole way of thinking about positive and negative feelings. It *won't* be all right in Hopkins' world. The pangs are schooled at forepangs, and all we can be thankful for is that each day dies with sleep. But we can also thank him for saying it, and understand that we can live vigorously in agony—and never hold that agony cheap.

CHAPTER SEVEN

Woman on a Quest

 QUESTION

Body my house
my horse my hound
what will I do
when you are fallen

Where will I sleep
How will I ride
What will I hunt

Where can I go
without my mount
all eager and quick
How will I know
in thicket ahead

is danger or treasure
when Body my good
bright dog is dead

How will it be
to lie in the sky
without roof or door
and wind for an eye

With cloud for shift
how will I hide?

MAY SWENSON

(1919–1989)

When we put a verb before a noun and surprise our-selves by turning a whole world on its head, we have discovered the way to understanding. Of course we are very young when we accomplish this special syntax of inversion. Quickly afterwards we learn to drive adults mad with constant queries. But when we become adults we use questions to drive *ourselves* mad—questions can be instruments of knowledge or torture. Not being able to ask them puts us under a repressive regime—we are infantilized, which is why we strenuously object to this stricture on our liberty.

With questions we investigate how the world was made, and we discover—gradually, maybe over a whole lifetime— that the world may not have been made to revolve around *us*. Thus, learning to question marks the very beginning of adulthood, even if we don't start asking truly introspective questions till much later on.

Among our first questions are those we address to our bodies. What's this? *A toe.* What's *this?* A penis. You might say bodies are the recipients of our most intense questions, first *and* last, since of course we ask them even more as we age. Answers, on the other hand, are formulated in ordinary word order. A's are statements, unlike inverted Q's. If all the world is a stage, just imagine countless starstruck statements waiting for their big chance—the casting call of a great question.

Great questions—the ones that cannot be answered simply—are at the heart of the circulatory system of the poem. They pump ideas of meaning through the lines, leading us to ambiguity and paradox and other ways of indirect knowing. Understanding indirectly, intuiting an answer, occurs when the system of the image conjures up a picture that the system of the sentence carries through the poem. Thus great questions may never be answered directly, but only connected, through the dovetailing of images, to intimate, intuitive understanding.

Questions that leave only images for answers can stymie us, but bafflement, too, is a method of growth. All groping is. Inchworms arriving at the ends of our branches, we poke the air for answers. And when we find our probings unsupported, then we attain the state of not knowing that becomes the only knowledge we have.

May Swenson, a poet who seemed to ride through life bareback, her hair flying, knew this condition very well. A reader has to look all the way to the bottom of her poem "Question" for a question mark, though the poem itself asks as insistently as a tugging child. At the same time, the poem is the consummate adult experience—if we define maturity as an awareness of our place in the universe. As a matter of fact, if we look down this poem, the question mark at the end is the *only* mark of punctuation. Oh dear. How do the sentences begin and end? And why is there punctuation as the finale when there's been none before? Why are some lines capitalized and others not? Isn't this *inconsistent*? Even the stanzas are uneven. "Question" became my talisman poem precisely because of these mysteries. I have to confess I even ignored the title on the first few readings, I was so captured by the strangeness of the opening lines:

Body my house
my horse my hound
what will I do
when you are fallen

Body my house is an odd construction. Something— either an "is" or a comma—has been left out. Living in a culture that divides mind from muscle at every opportunity, of course we know that a body can be a house—for the spirit. But by the second line the body also is a horse and a hound, a strange kind of trinity. Swenson puts the body over us *and* under us, while it follows us—at least its doggy shadow does. Her system of the line incorporates the sounds of her vocabulary and unifies the disparate things a body is with three alliterating "h"s. In fact, the words share so many similar letters they are almost confusing, except that a *horse*, a *house*, and a *hound* are resolutely separate, basic nouns we've known since we could speak. The poet constructs the lines in a childlike way—jamming four nouns together as if the line were built by a four-year-old pointing at pictures. She reminds us that poetry has been defined as the act of naming, that Adam, in Western culture, was deemed the first poet because he had the pleasure of naming the birds and beasts.

But if a child begins the naming, it is an adult who finishes the question:

what will I do
when you are fallen

Fallen, as in "fallen in battle," has a valiance to it, and it fits the horse best, though a house, too, can fall, taking a lineage with it, like the House of Usher, or the House of Atreus—or a house can literally fall in, as I once watched my own family house cave in under the wrecking ball. That house possessed a kind of valiance, like a brave horse, and a kind of unquestioning honesty, like a good dog. A delicious ambiguity is presented in the person of the pronoun "I." The *body* is **my** *house, horse,* and *hound,* where an "I" lives, yet the "I" is also the body, which in turn is the *house, horse,* and *hound.* And when they are fallen, so the "I" must, too.

Now, there's a three-car pileup of questions:

Where will I sleep
How will I ride
What will I hunt

The house, the horse, and the hound each get their own verb—*sleep, ride,* and *hunt*—and their own question signal—*Where, How,* and *What.* It's as if Swenson assigned herself to be the news reporter of her poem. But more strangeness in the system of the sentence creeps in under the journalistic style. You might be able to equate a horse with a hound, but a house is a great big inanimate *thing.* Logically we know that the three words don't all exist in the same category (animate vs. inanimate objects), but Swenson gives them equal weight because the house, horse, and hound are *grammatically* parallel. If you think of the poet as a painter, then Swenson composes a world by bringing three images of completely different proportions into the same plane, creating a special universe within the confines of the painting's two dimensions. By placing the nouns side by side by side without differentiation, then matching up three verbs to the parallel nouns, then plunking down three forms of inquiry—there! A rudimentary universe is born within a page's margins. All a *Body* needs to sustain its *house* is a *horse* and a *hound* for companionship and hunting up a dinner. Yet as soon as we perceive this blessedly simple universe, we know that it is deteriorating.

A childish desperation, a "but, but, but. . . ." comes into the voice as the poet realizes she will not be able to perform the tasks that ensure her survival—essential tasks that are also essential joys. A panic sets in, an anticipation of loss. At this point the poem always recalls for me the anxiety that throws its net over me whenever I try to prepare myself for the death of someone I love. A roiling fear says, "You'll never survive. What will you *do, do, do?*" I cannot answer it—and I try to flee the thought, but May Swenson stays. She persists with the inquisition, first with the horse:

> *Where can I go*
> *without my mount*
> *all eager and quick*

Eager and *quick* are the very first modifiers—ten lines down into the poem!—to appear. They make us realize how unadorned her writing has been so far. The house, horse, and hound have existed like toys on a vast polished wooden floor. *Eager* and *quick* let the horse chafe at its bit—

now quickened and alive. And because the adjectives breathe life into the nouns, the phrasing, or the syntax, changes. Why do adjectives animate nouns? Because each modifier is accompanied by an invisible grammatical "is." The structure of the language says, horse **is** *eager,* horse **is** *quick,* attaching states of being to the horse. And with two states of being, as well as a verb, the horse trots into three-dimensional life.

> *How will I know*
> *in thicket ahead*
> *is danger or treasure*

Like that of the opening two lines, this syntax is odd. It's almost like a dialect. Spoken by an early form of human? By a horse perhaps? Or a dog? Of course we understand what she means (how will I know if danger or treasure is ahead in that thicket), but if she stated it in traditional word order it would be flattened out, demystified, without its pulse.

A quickening pulse has been driving this poem as surely as the beat of hooves—the beat of its lines. In Swenson's musical system there are two words in each line that are louder than the others, like the clop of a horse's hooves. Look again at the second line, and you can pick them out: *horse* and *hound.* And in the third line: *what* and *I;* in the fourth, *you* and the first syllable of *fallen.* In the second stanza, you can hear the hoof land on the first and last words of each line, accenting *where/sleep, how/ride,* and *what/hunt.* And then in the oddball, dialect-like speech of the third stanza: *where/go, (with)out/mount, ea(ger)/quick, how/know* are louder than the other words. Every line has two unfailingly strong accents. They don't fall evenly, but they are surely there. It's not an overly even marching step, but a naturally regular, relaxed one-two: the mammal beat. The lope of a dog, the canter of the hunter—or even the creak and swell of a house, if you believe that houses are alive.

Can you *mount* panic? Is this what Swenson does with her mammal beat:

> *Is DANger or TREAsure*
> *when BOdy my GOOD*
> *bright DOG is DEAD*

Oh my God, Body is a *name*. Names are sculptural, kinesthetic, a kind of verbal touching. We are touched by the murmur of a name. And so we are moved by Body, the moniker of the good, bright dog. But the ambiguity of this poem is such that Body might be the poet's name as well. Now we are deep into the central nervous system of the poem, which sends out pictures for answers.

Names themselves evoke pictures. Think how much effort we put into them. Naming a pet exacts physical energy—thought upon thought. Giving a lover a pet name takes utmost care and balance. Think of the satisfaction you feel when the name is just right. It locates the soul. Soul, or *sawol*, is a completely English word, without known roots in another language. We find it in Old English records of sermons that distinguish between the body and the soul—the part of us that lives on after death. Names, of course, live on when we are gone, at least as long as someone *remembers our name*. If a name is soul-locating, then think what it means to call a being Body.

Body, all we have, protector and friend.

When we learn in the next line that Body is dead, we can hardly assimilate the information. We have just met Body! And now Body is gone. It is a devastating moment in the poem, and, even though I've read it many times, I'm never really prepared for it. Part of this devastation is the introduction of two adjectives (with their implied states of being). *Good* and *bright* subtly turn up the emotional volume. The superlatives are so simple, so unadorned themselves, that they break my heart with their ordinary praises.

Questions are a way of routing, a way of knowing *where* we are so we can learn *who* we are, and therefore name ourselves. But how do we get our bearings in the face of death? The steady triumvirate of *house-horse-hound* is unbalanced by the thought of the death of the dog. It's as if one leg of a triangle has been destroyed. The other two legs will collapse, and the geometry of the three-part universe will evaporate. Since thoughts of triangles lead to trinities,

I like to think of the dog as the Holy Ghost, the breath, or the spirit of life. After all, dog is God spelled backwards. . . . As the dog disappears, so Body in all its concepts (including that human body that lurks beneath the poem, the body of the speaker) vanishes. There is a first person speaking here, we must remember, though the pronoun "I" has been obscured by the confusion of the house, horse, and hound. (Or perhaps I should say a fusion.)

The next stanza whirls to the afterlife:

> *How will it be*
> *to lie in the sky*
> *without roof or door*
> *and wind for an eye*

By poem's end, that "I" lies in the sky, like a constellation, without a house (*roof or door*) and with *wind for an eye*, the wind that can blow right through you, right through your "I."

Reading this poem now, unwillingly anticipating these disembodied changes, I think of the constellation Orion, the hunter with his dog at his side, far above in the sky, always easy to find by the three stars of his sword. The animal spirits become *in*animate, stellar, and far away. May Swenson's appealingly childlike visual logic, which put both animate and inanimate in the same category, has shifted to a single flat plane. Like a children's verse, with its two-beat lines and the rhyme of *sky* and *eye*, the poet's plaint proceeds to *shift*.

> *With cloud for shift*
> *how will I hide?*

Think of the clouds as clothing, as a shift to dress a woman's body . . . or think of the shifting clouds, that would never be enough to cover a naked, exposed body. . . . Clouds themselves can shift, moving through the bodiless being in the sky. Maybe this shift is a shroud. . . .

Wind for an eye is a surprising and chilling idea because, although the wind makes its actual named appearance for the first time, it has been present as a sense of exhilaration before. The wind has rushed by the poet on her steed; the dog has stuck its nose in the wind. The house has shut its windows and doors against it. But now there *is* no eye, as there is no face on the constellation of the Hunter, and wind whistles through its nothingness.

May Swenson grew up in Utah and loved her girlhood in the West. She wrote a marvelous poem, "The Centaur," about a girl riding an imaginary horse—and that is a windy poem, far from the small apartment in New York City where she chose to live most of her adult life. Because of the childish diction in "Question," I can't help but connect it with Swenson's youth and "The Centaur," who, in that poem, is a little girl's evocation of the mythic half-human, half-horse. The girl is riding a willow branch she has cut with her brother's knife. (She says she has a whole stable of horses because of a willow grove.) The posture of her young body, at one with the imaginary horse, defines her pride in how she carries herself and in how successfully she carries off her fantasy. But the transformed figures of horse and hound tear at the boundaries of the self in "Question." I think of this poem as a portrait of Swenson's aging, and visualize her square face with its characteristic haircut—short bangs straight across the forehead, a bit of Buster Brown framing the strong-boned but weathered features.

How will I hide? The threat of exposure is so severe it is as if the poet could *die* of exposure. She reminds us how necessary it is to have a hiding place, that the hiding place— small as that apartment in Greenwich Village was in contrast to the Utah vastness—is the safety in which we grow. That stillness is as necessary to growth as questions are. I am reminded what slender means May Swenson had. She was a bootstrap poet, earning her way through the University of Utah and landing in New York with little in her pockets, working for the WPA, then at office jobs, as we learn from R. R. Knudson's biography, *The Pen of May Swenson.* I think of her quiet life as a kind of sustained hiding, a life-raft life that protected a place necessary to grow from and grope from. From that source she wrote poems of magnetic strangeness, creating a kind of touchstone pole, a true north.

On the umpteenth reading of the poem, I finally asked

myself about the title. Why did May Swenson call it "Question," singular? After all, it is eight questions, strung together. Yet the sole punctuation mark brings all eight together into the basic question: *How do we live and die?*

Is it through word order that we learn the order of the world? A question is, after all, a quest. The root is from the Latin *quaerere*, to ask, to seek. This poem—about the ultimate question, death—is both uprooted by our first childhood grappling with inversion and connected to imagination, since it is through imagination that we can invert a world. When you shake a person upside down, unexpected loose change falls out. Whenever the diction of childhood appears, it shakes out hope. Because of the merging of a child's way of speaking with the question of death, hope threads its way through Swenson's considering of the end of things. Inversion makes a readiness, an expectation of something next—and next is always exciting. Even death means the brink of a new world.

CHAPTER EIGHT

Sex Behind a Jeweled Curtain

 To the Tune
"Cutting a Flowering
Plum Branch"

Red lotus incense fades on
The jeweled curtain. Autumn
Comes again. Gently I open
My silk dress and float alone
On the orchid boat. Who can
Take a letter beyond the clouds?
Only the wild geese come back
And write their ideograms
On the sky under the full
Moon that floods the West Chamber.
Flowers, after their kind, flutter
And scatter. Water after

Its nature, when split, at last
Gathers again in one place.
Creatures of the same species
Long for each other. But we
Are far apart and I have
Grown learned in sorrow.
Nothing can make it dissolve
And go away. One moment,
It is on my eyebrows.
The next, it weighs on my heart.

LI CH'ING-CHAO

(1081–1140)

Translated by Kenneth Rexroth

A novel in a jewel box, a love affair in a single scene, the romance of Li Ch'ing-chao's poem "To the Tune 'Cutting a Flowering Plum Branch' " never shines too bright a light on its subject. This twelfth-century Chinese poem is full of cloaked sex and longing—just how discreetly sexual I discovered as a university administrator on my lunch hour, at the age of twenty-three. Eating an egg-salad sandwich in my office, without a grip on my fate, I gripped a book, *Love and the Turning Year, One Hundred More Poems from the Chinese*, translated by Kenneth Rexroth, and found this poet.

Seven years earlier I had not recognized the love of my life. I thought he was just my high school boyfriend. We were sixteen years old and virgins and had spent hours nuzzling each other and almost doing it. When we could suffer our bodies no more, we climbed from the backseat of the Chrysler and went out to haunt art galleries and bookstores. With Mike I bought my first books of poetry: the poets of Asia. After I graduated from college, I forsook both poetry and him, never dreaming that, just like the upset of the last line of a haiku, nineteen years later he would suddenly reappear, to become my husband, turning my life upside-down like a snowglobe.

But up in that unpoetic administrative tower, all I wanted was to be efficient. Yet like an errant satin bra strap, lines of poetry began slipping out onto the backs of the transfer credit forms I endlessly filled out. There in my office I had begun to think of myself as those Chinese magistrates who toiled for the government—when they were not exiled—but who had poems up their sleeves nonetheless.

The writer whom Rexroth called "The Poetess Li Ch'ing-chao" opened up a world of erotic detail to me—like an etching in which each pubic curl is a separate line. All her poems seem to take place in an atmosphere of sensuous languor. She builds "To the Tune 'Cutting a Flowering Plum Branch' " like an archipelago, its images surfacing like a string of islands across the page, and across time.

Red lotus incense fades on
The jeweled curtain. Autumn
Comes again. Gently I open
My silk dress and float alone
On the orchid boat.

Her technique, as Rexroth interprets it, is to use each of the five senses to build the string of images, and she begins with smell, the sense tied to both sexuality and memory: *Red lotus incense*. The burning smell conjures its source, the open red lotus on its lily pad. That flower looms as large as Georgia O'Keeffe's painting of the red poppy. When she turns the poem to the next sense, sight, *The jeweled curtain* sparkles behind vapors. It almost rattles slightly, on an invisible wind that the fading *incense* evokes. Then, kinesthetically, the poem wraps *Autumn* around us. Had it entered through that jeweled curtain? Next, the speaker *opens* her *silk dress*, that most sensuous article of exterior clothing, so suggestive is it of the silk of female interiors. Finally she *float[s] alone/On the orchid boat*.

Oh, I thought, drinking my ginger ale at my desk, she must be on a houseboat full of orchids. I thumbed to the back of the book. In the world of Chinese poetry, where every image conveys a secret thought, books of translations are always full of notes. *Orchid boat*, I learned, stood for female genitals, specifically, vulva.

I was reading a poem about masturbating.

"A poet is a failed painter," goes an old saying, and this is never more true than in a translation, where often *only* the pictures a poet has painted are conveyed. As a matter of fact, translations are ideal lenses through which to examine how imagery—the central nervous system of a poem— functions, because the other systems of the poem, the sentence and the line, can vaporize in the leap from language to language. This is especially true of translation from a language like Chinese, in which this poem was originally composed, to the standard tune "Cutting a Flowering Plum Branch" (a song whose rhythms are unknown to most Western readers) and written down—or, rather, brushstroked— as ideograms. Chinese calligraphy uses pictorial ideas. If it weren't for the replication or approximation of the image, the poem would remain untranslatable. Li Ch'ing-chao paints a picture of herself as if she were a character in her own story, her love story. And it is a remarkable tale because, contrary to all the strictures of her society, she married for love. However, in this poem she is alone—and makes love to herself in her partner's absence.

The way a pin dropping makes you know the depth of the silence you are experiencing, so masturbation, even when you have a nice, comforting orgasm, makes you know the depth of your aloneness in the world. When the poet asks, *Who can/Take a letter beyond the clouds?* we know that the answer is, *no one.* She has only the natural world to turn to.

Only the wild geese come back
And write their ideograms
On the sky under the full
Moon that floods the West Chamber.

The geese are skywriting. But they inscribe nothing but the ways of nature on the sky. The woman alone in the moonlit *West Chamber* lies in a solitude that crests into loneliness. The partner she evokes is all air, nothing but cloud and moonlight. The harvest moon presides over fall, the season of the end, of dying possibilities, of finishing the year, of aging, of a light going out, of life by oneself. . . . Surely the West Chamber had been their shared room.

How was it, I wondered in my office, that I rarely read a record of sexual life in a poem? Not just a dreamy reference, but a woman who actually opens her dress as she opens her—to use the Old English word for it—cunt. How much I wanted to write the way this woman was showing me (or, in fact, as Kenneth Rexroth created the way she was showing me). Unbeknownst to me at my paperwork, I was soon to be on my way through tumultuous life. I would travel a road through upheavals of family and friends and geography, of lovers, money, airports, automobiles, and apartments, of cities and fields and fate. In fact, I was already on that road, though I didn't know it. My metal desk was just a way station—far, far from the boudoir of a poet-concubine. That's what I thought Li Ch'ing-chao was at the time.

Later on I learned by reading the notes of the scholar Ling Chung, with whom Kenneth Rexroth worked, that Li Ch'ing-chao was not a courtesan at all. She was the beloved daughter of a family of scholars, a bold child who dared to write poetry all on her own and even to express social and political thoughts in it. We probably cannot know the depth of how radical it was in twelfth-century China for her family to indulge her playful brilliance, but they did, and in time she became a scholar and a poet and fell in love with a young scholar from a prominent political family. Her husband, Chao Ming-ch'eng, also wrote poetry, though it was she who was the truly brilliant artist. And they had other passions in common: music, calligraphy, and collecting antiquities. The two began their collection in the cozy joy of their love match. Here is what Li Ch'ing-chao writes of the idyll of their first days together:

My husband was twenty-one then, studying at the Imperial Academy. Both the Chao and the Li families were not wealthy. Our lives had been modest and thrifty. On the first and the fifteenth of each month, when he was granted leave of absence from school, he used to pawn his clothes for five hundred copper coins so that he could buy fruit and rubbings of stone inscriptions in the market at the Hsiang Kao Temple. After he brought them home, the two of us would taste the fruit and study the rubbings. We enjoyed ourselves

so much that we claimed ourselves the citizens of the ancient ideal state of Ko Tien.
From *Li Ch'ing-chao: Complete Poems,* translated and edited by Kenneth Rexroth and Ling Chung

Years before, I'd taken drives with my then high school boyfriend Mike, playing vocabulary games and arguing about books and kissing and laughing so hard we spilled root beer on the dashboard . . . How unromantic that sounds compared to the pawning of the young man's clothes. And yet I felt I understood the young poet and her husband completely.

But lolling in an American suburb, I was clueless about what it must have been like for this couple to be caught in the power struggles of the imperial court. Both the Li and the Chao families fell in and out of political favor. At one point Li Ch'ing-chao was forced to write poems beseeching her father-in-law, who was in power, to rescue her father, whose politics had caused him to be cast out. After her father was saved, her in-laws fell from favor, and her husband was arrested and interrogated. Then the couple were banished to the provinces, where—this will not seem odd to anyone who seeks a quiet life—they lived happily for ten years. Here she writes in the third person of their life together:

Every evening after dinner, they sat together and played a game they had invented themselves in front of a pile

*of books. The game consisted of pointing out in which
volume, on which page, and in which line such or such
an event was mentioned. The one who guessed correctly
was the winner and had the privilege of taking a sip of
jasmine tea. Sometimes they enjoyed themselves so im-
mensely and laughed so much that they caused the tea
cup to tumble from their lips.*

During these years, Li Ch'ing-chao and Chao Ming-
ch'eng collected ten huge rooms full of paintings, calligraphy, ceremonial vessels, and stone rubbings, building one of
the great ancient collections of even more ancient antiquities. But in the ups and downs of their political fortunes,
almost all this collection was lost, and Li Ch'ing-chao endured many separations from her husband and finally a life
alone as his widow. It was not an existence of calm and solitude—it was full of still more political tumult and a later
marriage and divorce. How modern a life she led. Her
poems, in contrast, exist without a hint of struggle.

Or is it only a surface of calm?

*Flowers, after their kind, flutter
And scatter.*

There is the image of dispersal that is the fall season, but
considering her life, this must also have meant the dispersal of war and of her great collection, and thus the disper-

sal of beauty and the scattering of love. The fluttering motion visually echoes how the flowers of the plum tree scatter as a branch is cut, the name of the melody that accompanies this poem (a song we never hear as we read the poem in translation). But immediately she consoles us for this loss with an image of joining:

> *Water after*
> *Its nature, when spilt, at last*
> *Gathers again in one place.*

Though at last there will be a gathering, there is no gathering *now.* Now the loneliness exists in the pure space of the beloved's absence. . . . That indentation of the pillow where the other's head has lain. That T-shirt we cannot wash because we dare not lose the smell . . . The flower and water images lead to the *Creatures of the same species* who *Long for each other.* This longing, the poet says, is as much what it means to be human as scattering is what it means to be a petal, and pooling what it means to be water.

The central nervous system is "the primary center for the regulation and control of bodily activities," my *American Heritage Dictionary,* third edition, says, "receiving and interpreting sensory impulses." When we talk about the vision of a poet, even when we call someone *visionary,* we refer to the image that sustains the vision. Even in—especially in—a translation sustained through time and through the deeply

estranged syntaxes of English and Chinese, the vision of the
poet retains its unity because of imagery. Imagery is largely
built of nouns. When all else fails you in reading a poem, you
can always read the nouns aloud and free-associate among
them. The nouns will always give you a basic idea of where
the poet is going. Try this list: *incense, curtain, autumn, dress,
orchid boat, letter, clouds, geese, ideograms, sky, moon, chamber,
flowers, water, creatures, we, I, sorrow, nothing, eyebrows, heart.*
The progress of thought becomes clear as we look to the
center of each image. The noun is there, like the pupil of the
eye of the poet. The single noun is *what* the poet sees, and
the collection of nouns in a poem is *how* the poet sees. This
is what we mean when we talk about a poet's vision.

Following the nouns through the next two sentences
delivers the blow of the lover's absence, from *we* to *I*, from
sorrow to *nothing*.

> But *we*
> Are far apart and I have
> Grown learned in sorrow.
> Nothing can make it dissolve
> And go away.

The knowledge that there is no cure for the beloved's
absence, yet the attempt to go on curing by evoking the
love and through the consolation of making that love to
herself, creates the heavy weight of the closing lines. The se-

quential position of the nouns, *moment, eyebrows, heart,* literally marks the progression of Li Ch'ing-chao's emotional adjustment.

> *One moment,*
> *It is on my eyebrows.*
> *The next, it weighs on my heart.*

The poem evokes, delicately, all mental activity with *eyebrow*—poised in the face, that recording realm of the senses. In fact, this completely physical poem has proceeded from the orchid boat to the eyebrow to the heart. Head, heart, and sex—that is all of us, complete. Love, she implies, is the sensuous apprehension of the universe, and being in love creates a universe in which to live. The struggle of loneliness is all the ways in which we attempt to create that universe of love, including touching our own organs, recognizing *what* we are, so that we may know *who* we are in the absence of the mirror of the beloved who, in the past, so easily reflected us.

In my office I found the physical reality of a twelfth-century woman so intimate that I rose to shut my door. Behind that door, I waited for my life to begin. And later, as I left that sterile room and cut away from that town, I kept "To the Tune 'Cutting a Flowering Plum Branch' " with me. Eventually I wrote my own sensuous poem about masturbating and put it in a book I called *Raw Heaven.* When

Mike saw a review of that book nineteen years after we broke up, he wrote me a letter that would renew our relationship. That letter seemed to come from *beyond the clouds*.

Perhaps to hold up a love poem as a map for the mystery of how another love relationship would progress is just too much. It's a poem, after all, not a horoscope, not a tarot card. But other people's visions do point the way through life. That is why we look for them. They model ways of being and, even when they describe a weight on the heart, are a consolation. That is why lovers search for poems for each other. It is never just to put our feelings into words. It is to add another's vision to our own. Even if you can't count yourself among the most articulate of beings, someone else's words will make you fly. Or sigh. You can enter the universe of someone else's love and meet your own loving within it, a community of lovers, a love circle.

CHAPTER NINE

A
Bedtime Story

 ### TALKING
IN BED

Talking in bed ought to be easiest,
Lying together there goes back so far,
An emblem of two people being honest.

Yet more and more time passes silently.
Outside, the wind's incomplete unrest
Builds and disperses clouds about the sky,

And dark towns heap up on the horizon.
None of this cares for us. Nothing shows why
At this unique distance from isolation

It becomes still more difficult to find
Words at once true and kind,
Or not untrue and not unkind.

PHILIP LARKIN

(1922–1985)

When I first read the title "Talking in Bed," I thought of the most intimate moments of prone conversation, just after lovemaking and just before sleep. My parents, who spent their daylight hours in arguments, talked cozily in bed late at night, their cigarettes flashing in the dark. My grandparents gossiped through the wee hours under their quilts. And when I was old enough to fall asleep with a like-minded person, I relished emitting these end-of-day murmurs and hearing another's sleepy replies.

So imagine my disappointment at the silence between this couple in Philip Larkin's poem. Because it is about *trying* to talk in bed (or trying not to blurt out something terrible), this poem is about a discipline of self-control that ought not to have to be practiced in intimate spaces—yet is, routinely, in many bedrooms all over the world. It points to the fact that some of us live outer lives entirely different from our innermost ones. Our exteriors are gruff strangers to our interiors. Our protective fronts shield us from casual affronts, and sometimes our exteriors even work to affront the world. Larkin, who no doubt would have favored Grumpy of all the seven dwarfs, knew that giving a slight undercoating of negativity coats the world in a protective gray—shielding us from the worst by expecting less.

Thus, "Talking in Bed" is about a subject taboo on the North American continent—disappointment. After all, we are supposed to have everything. But, of course, people in the middle of their lives and in the middle of their marriage bed often find themselves in the middle of a quandary—how to be decent to the other person and still be honest? Every evening a special preemptive war is waged in battered old relationships—to keep silent the words that should never be spoken yet still to communicate to the one who, sharing our bed, must also share our lives. It's not surprising that "Talking in Bed" is a Cold War poem. Philip Larkin, a British poet from the era of John Le Carré's spy George Smiley, took disappointment as an appropriate postwar subject. So why did I bother, looking for a poem about cozy talk, to persist with this one about disappointment, settling on the voice of a notorious grump? Well, that is a story we can hold to one side, just as I was holding carefully to my side of a bed I was unfortunately sharing, lying stiffly wide awake in the middle of the night. . . .

There's a way in which I, child of the Cold War, learned about disappointment from Larkin, a Cold War adult. To explain why you are grumpy in a happy society requires you to be discriminating. This calls for adjectives, perfect adjectives, and Larkin is the champion of that ill-used part of speech. After all, his enterprise requires the fine sifting of description to get at *exactly* what is. It's his job to slice everyday living into an onion-skin layer of cells thin enough to be slid onto the slide that he will then slip under his lens.

Talking in bed ought to be easiest, he begins, then gives the reason:

> *Lying together there goes back so far,*
> *An emblem of two people being honest.*

Yet Larkin, who knows very well the distance between what we'd like to blurt out and what we actually say, understands that this emblem of honesty is bound to produce a "yet."

Yet begins the next stanza. *Yet more and more time passes silently.* This is the only place in the poem where the system of the line exactly matches the system of the sentence. Whenever these two systems coincide, their two independent rhythms suddenly join, and a special bell of recognition seems to ring in the poem. Here that bell notes the dramatic shift between what is supposed to be and what is. Rhythmically, we hear an interior "pop" as if the poet were a chiropractor, giving his opening stanza an adjustment, realigning the spine of meaning with that *yet*. People *ought* to talk honestly in bed, but now *time passes silently.* (Better to say nothing . . . this half of the couple thinks.)

Having described the interior atmosphere, Larkin moves to chart the exterior. Readers don't think of Larkin as a landscape artist because we are so used to following his social eye, but he is like a medieval Flemish painter, spreading brilliantly detailed scenery from an upper-story window.

Outside, the wind's incomplete unrest
Builds and disperses clouds about the sky,

And dark towns heap up on the horizon.

The towns are *dark* and the wind both *builds* and *disperses* the clouds. As the weather shifts, the degrees of darkness in Larkin's palette separate and intensify, and Larkin prepares us grammatically for a crucial distinction he will make later on. He calls the wind's unrest *incomplete* using *un-* and *in-* to shade the wind's activity into subtler meaning. Both *in-* and *un-* negate nouns and adjectives, just as *not* negates the verbs of Gerard Manley Hopkins' sonnet "No Worst." The noun or adjective still has its root—here the roots are "complete" and "rest"—and still carries the cherished, positive meaning of the roots: complete rest. But the prefixes *in-* and *un-* disturb the perfect roots so that the rest becomes rest*less.* Now a delicate upheaval happens— suddenly we realize that what is out the window is actually the mental landscape of the inhabitants of that bed who have been *lying together there*. The *dark towns* that have built *up on the horizon* are the dark thoughts that have built up between the two people, thoughts that could be translated into lies for those who have been *lying . . . there*. The double meaning of the homophone "lie" subtly hovers over us as we view them.

Who are these people? I'm surprised to say I've always imagined them to be Larkin's parents, though certainly one could be Larkin himself. Why his parents? Because there is such a long-term settled distance between them, and because the point of view of the poem is both closely observed *and* from a distance—as one might view one's parents.

When Larkin discloses that *None of this cares for us. Nothing shows why . . .* the ultimate negations of *None* and *Nothing* create a ghost of caring, a sense that we were cared for once, but no longer. This makes the sense of vacancy all the more terrible—and more poignant—because it refers so distantly, but so intimately, to figures in bed. The scenery has a life of its own and turns its back on us, even as it pervades our midst and is the symbol of our interior life. Wind and sky are *nature* and go their own ways. They cannot be personified. Silent themselves, they can't be made to sympathize with the silence between these two in bed. Nor can the distant towns that *heap up*. They are just a pile of architecture, boxy blocks without human dimension that offer no human comfort. The outside neither pays attention to us nor shows *why/At this unique distance from isolation* . . . What unique distance? Which isolation? Larkin must be referring to the unique distance of inches between the two in bed, meaning their closeness. However, the psychological impact of a word like *isolation* and the use of that noun *distance* in a situation of intimacy—and all the intimacy any adult ever hopes for is there in the picture of two heads on their pillows—insert the uncertain dark landscape between them. Can't you imagine their faces? Though they are close, they are as closed to each other as if they had already shut their eyes. By using the language of landscape, Larkin takes the exterior world—the exterior world that is neutral at best, or uncaring, or without reason—and plunges it in between those two people in bed. The schism between the exterior and interior seems unbridgeable. The social reality of the Cold War was that two superpowers occupied the great bed of the political world, unable to talk to each other.

> *Nothing shows why*
> *At this unique distance from isolation*
>
> *It becomes still more difficult to find*

Whatever made talking in bed *easiest* in the first line has become by the tenth line *still more difficult*.

Now that we've recalled that word *easiest*, it might be

nice to look at the system of the sentence and follow the rhyme scheme through the poem. Rhyme schemes can be keys to secrets in a poem, since rhymes are often like little padlocks at the ends of lines. *Easiest* rhymes with *honest*— but what do we do with *far?* Nothing else rhymes with that. Then *unrest* pops up in the middle of the second stanza, to rhyme with *easiest* and *honest*. When you see three lines and find a rhyme from the first stanza poking its head out in the second, you may be in the presence of Dante's favorite rhyme scheme, *terza rima*. This is a knitting of rhyme that connects the stanzas by passing through them like a needle looping wool. Traditionally, it goes aba, bcb, cdc, etc. Of course Larkin doesn't do it quite that way. He grabs the formal idea and gives it a shadow function in the poem. All poets appropriate verse forms for their own devices. (Even in prosody there is poetic license.) Larkin lets *far* wag out in the air, happily unrhymed, then picks up a kind of braiding action by bringing *unrest* down to the next stanza, where he makes a loose sight-rhyme of *silently* and *sky*. This sound weaves into the third stanza with *why*. Then two delicious new near-rhymes come up with *horizon* and *isolation*.

Usually we think of *terza rima* as building and linking ideas together with sound, a merging of the systems of the sentence and the line. But by not always linking, Larkin can make the middle sound in the first three stanzas (*far, unrest,* and *why*) intrude on the other two sounds that are just *lying together there* in their stanzas. The third sound comes between them, just as the psychological reality of the dark landscape comes between the couple in the bed—or as ideology came between the East and the West.

Is this idea too neat to be true? Can I actually be saying that Larkin had this in mind when he wrote the poem in *terza rima?* Poetic thinking does have this nearly unbelievable aspect—it is so unlike the other types of thinking we do. The links between the three systems of a poem—the line, the sentence, and the image—are simultaneously rational *and* intuitive. In poetry, the left brain knows what the right brain is doing. Let's say that if Larkin didn't have these ideas centrally in mind, he had them peripherally in mind. (Another way to think about all these manifestations of social isolation is purely emotionally. Anyone who's ever lain on a therapist's couch—that's a form of talking in bed, isn't it?—knows that where the unconscious is concerned, the unrelated, eventually, is related to *everything.*)

In the company of reason and intuition, both functioning side by side (a power marriage, if the poem is working), surprising complexities evolve, each bolstering the other. And this happens in the last stanza, where suddenly there are three rhymes in a row. Often a salvo of rhymes ends a *terza rima*–type poem, because a cluster of the same sounds gives the lines a closure. In the case of this poem, though, the linking has been a form of interrupting. What ought to have been *easiest* has turned out to be *still more difficult.* So the three rhymes in the last stanza become a way of annealing, sealing, or even healing the ruptures.

The linked sounds are the bed in which the ghosts of negativity lie:

> *It becomes still more difficult to find*
> *Words at once true and kind,*

It is tough, lying there, to find something decent to say that won't belie our angers and years-long resentments and frustrations but will, at the same time, gesture toward the other person, acknowledging that person's role in the two-step of a long relationship. We feel we must preserve some honesty and extend some healing generosity to the other person.

This is where the *un*-words have their say, making ghosts of the positive:

> *Or not untrue and not unkind.*

"Not true" of course makes a statement false, as "Not kind" verges into cruel. But here the double negatives of *not* un*true and not* un*kind* make a complex, delicately true statement—a statement precise because of its subtly defined borders. The task of the couple is to locate these borders, to find the language that at least doesn't lie, although it doesn't tell the whole truth, and at least isn't cruel, because it soothes what it reveals.

We have all tried to soften truth but not to falsify, knowing that falsehood will destroy a relationship, yet knowing that shining too honest a light can destroy the relationship as well. It exacts a huge outlay of energy to lie in that bed, tempering our nasty sharpness by turning toward the other, inserting what we think is the other's perspective into our own so that we might say, *not* just anything, but the words that will both link and retain some clear signal that we really are our human selves, even as we lie entwined.

We are *far* from truth and kindness as we lie there. Even before the first stanza the Pollyanna language of romance was abandoned. But we are equally *far* from meanness and lies. The inverted negativity veils the truth by revealing its strategy. It makes the inner feelings surface into the outer demeanor.

True and *kind* as well as *untrue* and *unkind* are adjectives, those supposedly unnecessary parts of speech, those "mere" modifiers. Modifiers belong to civility; being civil requires accommodation, modification. And that sort of compromise always involves a personal ceding, or loss.

Do poems actually teach us how to be? Only by sheer demonstration. When behavior is modeled, it is outlined for us; we see it clearly. When we see our ways clear, we do come to some understanding, and that is a kind of teaching. Not all poems instruct in the way "Talking in Bed" does. But insofar as poems like this make subtle behavior distinctly clear, they clarify events in our own lives and make our thoughts and memories newly apparent to us as we carry the poem around. I'd never handled any of my disappointments civilly, I realized when I first really considered this poem. I had an audiotape of Philip Larkin reading "Talking in Bed" in his surprisingly lively, reedy but grumpy voice. I played it over and over on my Walkman in the middle of the night next to a figure on the other side of the bed with whom I couldn't talk. I didn't know why I was having such trouble sleeping! What was wrong with me, and why was I listening to Larkin, Larkin, Larkin? I could not admit that this relationship was falling apart. I kept looking for the words that would be not untrue and not unkind, but all the words I had were true and cruel or false and nice. In our arguments I ricocheted between these poles. I never attained a civil middle. My disappointment was huge and adolescent and demanding. I wasn't grown-up about what I wanted at all. How I needed that bed to be empty. Finally I harangued the other occupant out of it. . . . Of course, learning how to read a poem is not the same as learning how to live a life. . . . For me, though, reading a poem *is* living a life.

Alone at last, I reveled in having my own bed to myself—I was, it turned out, a child of the '60s and not much of a cold warrior, after all. Even though I didn't take the image of the couple in bed to heart, I took Larkin as my companion. With him, I never had to be Happy, I could be Grumpy. Grumpy fans fancy themselves realists, even though most of us are romantic slobs. This is a secret we never reveal, certainly not to ourselves. In Larkin's company I could both take a dim view of the world and protect myself from its vicissitudes. He makes his way in a kind of bereaved irony—giving his reader the sour courage to see if not easily, then not uneasily.

CHAPTER TEN

Letters from Two Fathers

 ## My Father's Loveletters

On Fridays he'd open a can of Jax,
Close his eyes, & ask me to write
The same letter to my mother
Who sent postcards of desert flowers
Taller than a man. He'd beg her
Return & promised to never
Beat her again. I was almost happy
She was gone, & sometimes wanted
To slip in something bad.
His carpenter's apron always bulged
With old nails, a claw hammer
Holstered in a loop at his side
& extension cords coiled around his feet.

Words rolled from under
The pressure of my ballpoint:
Love, Baby, Honey, Please.
We lingered in the quiet brutality
Of voltage meters & pipe threaders,
Lost between sentences . . . the heartless
Gleam of a two-pound wedge
On the concrete floor.
A sunset in the doorway
Of the tool shed.
I wondered if she'd laugh
As she held them over a flame.
My father could only sign
His name, but he'd look at blueprints
& tell you how many bricks
Formed each wall. This man
Who stole roses & hyacinth
For his yard, stood there
With eyes closed & fists balled,
Laboring over a simple word,
Opened like a fresh wound, almost
Redeemed by what he tried to say.

YUSEF KOMUNYAKAA

(b.1947)

127

LETTERS & OTHER WORLDS

'for there was no more darkness for him and, no doubt like Adam
before the fall, he could see in the dark'

My father's body was a globe of fear
His body was a town we never knew
He hid that he had been where we were going
His letters were a room he seldom lived in
In them the logic of his love could grow

My father's body was a town of fear
He was the only witness to its fear dance
He hid where he had been that we might lose him
His letters were a room his body scared

He came to death with his mind drowning.
On the last day he enclosed himself
in a room with two bottles of gin, later
fell the length of his body
so that brain blood moved
to new compartments
that never knew the wash of fluid
and he died in minutes of a new equilibrium.

His early life was a terrifying comedy
and my mother divorced him again and again.
He would rush into tunnels magnetized
by the white eye of trains
and once, gaining instant fame,
managed to stop a Perahara in Ceylon
—the whole procession of elephants dancers
local dignitaries—by falling
dead drunk onto the street.
As a semi-official, and semi-white at that,
the act was seen as a crucial
turning point in the Home Rule Movement
and led to Ceylon's independence in 1948.

(My mother had done her share too—
her driving so bad
she was stoned by villagers
whenever her car was recognized)

For 14 years of marriage
each of them claimed he or she
was the injured party.
Once on the Columbo docks
saying goodby to a recently married couple
my father, jealous
at my mother's articulate emotion,
dove into the waters of the harbour

and swam after the ship waving farewell.
My mother pretending no affiliation
mingled with the crowd back to the hotel.

Once again he made the papers
though this time my mother
with a note to the editor
corrected the report —saying he was drunk
rather than broken hearted at the parting of friends.
The married couple received both editions
of The Ceylon Times when their ship reached Aden.

And then in his last years
he was the silent drinker
the man who once a week
disappeared into his room with bottles
and stayed there until he was drunk
and until he was sober.

There speeches, head dreams, apologies,
the gentle letters, were composed.
With the clarity of architects
he would write of the row of blue flowers
his new wife had planted,
the plans for electricity on the house,
how my half-sister fell near a snake
and it had awakened and not touched her.
Letters in a clear hand of the most complete empathy

his heart widening and widening and widening
to all manner of change in his children and friends
while he himself edged
into the terrible acute hatred
of his own privacy
till he balanced and fell
the length of his body
the blood entering
the empty reservoir of bones
the blood searching in his head without metaphor

MICHAEL ONDAATJE

(b. 1943)

Using a stubby pencil and the back of a piece of sand-paper, my father wrote lists of what to get at the hardware store. I don't think I ever saw him write a letter. I think of my dad, of course, when I read these poems by Yusef Komunyakaa and Michael Ondaatje, because their poems speak what their fathers could not make known. Of course I know perfectly well that father-son relationships are very different from father-daughter relationships, and that class and race as well as gender separate me as a reader from these writers—but not, in these particular cases, too much. For me, these two poems are an argument for the particular, especially for the wrenching specifics each writer uses to create a tone of burden and love. Poetry, after all, is responsible for articulation, no matter how small or opaque or ephemeral the articulated thing is. I would go so far as to say that it articulates culture itself—provided we know a culture by the rhythms of its details.

In each of these poems the mom has left or divorced the dad. Both fathers have something they cannot say. Both sons feel the burden of bringing to brightly detailed speech the blurred interior qualities of their fathers' lives. Like my own dad, both fathers drink. But these two men use alcohol for inspiration, each closeting himself weekly in a ritual place, fabricating letters to fend off regret—in Komunyakaa's case, letters which the son actually has to write for the father. And both poems are about a kind of redemption, or at least about settling a roiled-up feeling. Interestingly, when both fathers are at their best, up pops flower and garden imagery.

When the collected details of a poem create a whole network of human habits, then the poem creates culture both by being part of it and by reflecting it. "My Father's Loveletters" is made from carefully extracted details, like the mother's postcards of desert flowers. (Are they flowers of desertion? They're prickly things at any rate, unpickable, and *taller than a man*. She looms over her ex-husband and her son.) Fridays are important—workweek's end, time for a beer and the ritual of this letter. This is a circular poem, appropriate for a ritual like theirs which returns at workweek's end. The opening image of the father's closed eyes—his unseeingness, his blind concentration—returns in the end, making the poem like the mythic Greek *uroboros*, the snake which bites its tail, creating a ring. That image of the head meeting the tail, a unifying circularity, operates behind the structures of both Ondaatje's and Komunyakaa's poems, but does so more starkly in "My Father's Loveletters" because of the opening and closing images. The system of imagery, the central nervous system of the poem, creates this *uroboros* with a single picture: the father's shut lids. Does the father refuse to see? Maybe we should say that the father refuses to look out, *for with eyes closed and fists balled* he turns inward.

The nervous system wires this poem with images: *postcards, tools, a ballpoint pen, extension cords, voltage meters, a concrete floor.* . . . The poem *is* concrete in its imagery, so vivid the other systems seem eclipsed by the system of the image, as they do in Marilyn Nelson's poem "Women's Locker Room," or Margaret Atwood's poem, "Asparagus." Free verse often flaunts its visual images, using the nervous system of the poem to lead a reader, submerging the importance of the musical system and the system of the sentence, although they are still quietly there.

One of the things to pay attention to in an unassuming-sounding free verse poem is the short lines. (Again, free verse means that there isn't a regular meter or rhyme scheme.) The opening lines range from eight to ten syllables in length. Then the short line happens, six syllables, coming just at the point of an emotional shift: *to slip in something bad.*

On Fridays he'd open a can of Jax,
Close his eyes, & ask me to write
The same letter to my mother
Who sent postcards of desert flowers
Taller than a man. He'd beg her
Return & promised to never
Beat her again. I was almost happy
She was gone, & sometimes wanted
To slip in something bad.

In the eight lines before this short line, the father asks the boy to write his words for him. But those adult words are like the beggings and promisings of a child—or at least of a man who is desperate. *He'd beg her/Return & promised to never/Beat her again.* The tall father lowers himself to the height of the little boy who takes on the task of begging for him. The man is diminished in the very act that bends his son with the burden of being taller than he can really be, taking on the grown-up act before he is ready. When the first personal pronoun "I" appears, Komunyakaa admits, *I was almost happy/She was gone.* Their lives must be a lot calmer now that they are alone. Because his parents are separated, the boy can be so grown-up as to take the responsibility of writing those love letters, just like a man— only of course he isn't. The boy becomes a diminutive version of the speaker in Gerard Manley Hopkins' "No Worst," feeling that he cannot ask Mother Mary for relief. So, as a boy without a mother, Komunyakaa's speaker wants

To slip in something bad. The shorter line downshifts the poem to a lower gear, so that the boy's rejection of his mother can sink in, and readers can feel his possession, through and through, of his dad.

Though the father's hammer is like a pistol, *Holstered in a loop at his side*, it is his son who fires, *under/The pressure of [his] ballpoint*, words the boy has no business writing, his father's sweet talk: *Love, Baby, Honey, Please.* Unspeaking, symbolic *voltage meters* register the electricity of this ritual, and *pipe threaders* unify disparate elements, estranged as the parents themselves.

When Komunyakaa says, *Lost between sentences*, I can't help thinking about life sentences. The father is sentenced to his illiteracy, and the boy is sentenced to speech. Poets do, of course, speak for other people. We want them to. They are the ones we run to for the essential words we need at funerals, weddings, anniversaries. In a way, this poem shows Komunyakaa in training for his later career.

But as a boy he is helpless against the wedge between his parents:

> *. . . the heartless*
> *Gleam of a two-pound wedge*
> *On the concrete floor.*

On the concrete floor is another of those half lines that pull the poem up short; so is *Of the tool shed*, which ends with a period, making a deep pause as the sun sets on this

135

scene, recalling the shed at sunset in Kenyon's "Let Evening Come." Images themselves are silent. What activates "word pictures" in a poem is that words make sounds. The heartbreaking punch comes from the overlay of image and music: as we see the image evoked, we hear the internal thud of our realization. Feeling is harnessed by Komunyakaa's coordination of line rhythm and visual frame. After the poem's longest sentence comes its shortest. Inside a sentence fragment without a verb, without motion, in a freeze frame, is the place where masculinity is forged. It is their womb, where the father and son linger *in the quiet brutality.* By saying *quiet* Komunyakaa makes us realize that brutality is usually noisy, but here it is silent—or inarticulate. The half line *Of the tool shed* triggers the reappearance of the mother like a storybook witch, burning the letters: *I wondered if she'd laugh/As she held them over a flame.*

Like his father, Komunyakaa stacks images brick by brick.

> *My father could only sign*
> *His name, but he'd look at blueprints*
> *& tell you how many bricks*
> *Formed each wall. This man*
> *Who stole roses & hyacinth*
> *For his yard, stood there*
> *With eyes closed & fists balled,*
> *Laboring over a simple word,*

Opened like a fresh wound, almost
Redeemed by what he tried to say.

If Komunyakaa had not used the unobtrusive adverb *almost* before he wrote *Redeemed*, then we would have to swallow the idea that his father's apologies erased the way he behaved. That's not true, of course. Words *don't* erase. Meaningful words are indelible—they are things you can't take back. Philip Larkin makes his whole poem "Talking in Bed" about this very problem. Nor can the father in Komunyakaa's poem take back the actions that drove away his wife—his son's mother. Yet in the speaking of his words—and in his son's writing of them—he is near redemption, perhaps as near as a modern human being can get—or at least a complex, intensely portrayed being such as this one.

Part of the subtle power of *almost* is its placement at the end of the line. Free verse depends on its breaks, where the line stops the sentence from going on and makes us pause—and therefore guess at—the next word. When the word is a surprise, that break succeeds, since most reading depends on predictability. Our lives are not only filled with predictable combinations, they are made of them—these combinations are the fabric of our daily communication. So if a writer says "green," we fill in the next words with something like "grass." But poetry depends on disturbing the predictable by being more accurate than we normally are—and therefore surprising and satisfying. Why? Because the inadequacy of what we normally predict is not only disclosed but gratifyingly replaced with what we come to think of as "the real truth."

For a moment, when the poem began its ending with the father's *eyes closed & fists balled*—which sounds so closed to "bawled" because the poem is so close to crying—I didn't remember the father's closed eyes in the beginning. Sometimes the *uroboros* evokes not only the circle but the *vicious* circle, and there is a way that the father cycles through violence to regret to apology, and a way that the Friday-night ritual grinds like a mill wheel at both the participants. The circularity of the poem, where the head of the snake recognizes the tail, closes the ritual; that ritual is not something that you can get out of—except, perhaps, by becoming a poet. Every Friday the fresh wound is opened again. Is the father laboring over finding a word to dictate to the boy? Laboring over signing his name? Or laboring over one word when the son has access to many, so many he became a poet, in order to name these feelings and thus to stop an agony of frustrated silence? It's nice to think here about the ampersand, the symbol for "and." Komunyakaa uses nine of them, visually evoking and reinforcing the circular links of the poem. Typographically, an ampersand has the snakelike quality of a symbol about to form the *uroboros:* & becoming O.

Circles are by definition unbroken—we don't know where these most whole of geometrical forms begin and end—and therefore we use rings to mean "forever." Parent-child relationships, whatever the attempts to sever them, endure forever, surely past the death of the parent, who lives on, ingested, inside the child, as the child was once contained in that parent's zygote. Circular poems of course aren't true rings, because they do have beginnings and end-ings. All articulation begins and ends somewhere. Yet when the end of a poem refers you to the beginning, and when the end of a poem is constructed like the beginning, then its circularity is inescapable. And we don't want to escape it. We all seem to like circles. I have never met anyone who didn't see the magic of a ring or didn't like to be held in an embrace, provided it was loose enough. . . . Letters, even the letters of the alphabet, have a linking, ringlike quality. Correspondence, if it is intense enough, is circular, unending. The sadness of Komunyakaa's father's love letters is that they aren't circular. The mother seems to have no intention of responding.

Michael Ondaatje's circular poem begins and ends with songlike chants about his father's letters. There is no punctuation in the songs; punctuation is left for the narra-tive that they surround. The beginning lines are openly singsong: *My FAther's BOdy WAS a GLOBE of FEAR/His BOdy WAS a TOWN we NEver KNEW.* The predictabil-ity of the alternating soft (unstressed) and loud (stressed) syllables helps us to understand the strangeness of the statements about the father's emotional life because the regularity of the pulse tames the wildness of the surreal statements. In the town that was the father, letters were a special room. Ondaatje, in this poem, is on his way to becoming a man of letters, a man inhabiting the room where the father was most alive, most himself—and most hidden from his family. *He hid that he had been where we were going.* The father wouldn't disclose his own patterns of growth, leaving the son rudderless.

Punctuation, which belongs to the system of the sentence, puts a shape to things, and punctuation in this poem begins only with the father's death. Life narratives are often conceived backwards because it's only when we come to an end that we can look back and construct the story of what happened. Death, the end point, shapes the life that went before it. Until death, the lived life can seem shapeless—we don't know the ultimate lines of the journey—but the period, the punctuation at the end of the life sentence, creates the point where a story can begin. That is the ring that articulation makes. *He came to death with his mind drowning,* Ondaatje tells us. Then we hear the half-real, half-metaphorical circumstances:

> *On the last day he enclosed himself*
> *in a room with two bottles of gin, later*
> *fell the length of his body*

so that brain blood moved
to new compartments
that never knew the wash of fluid
and he died in minutes of a new equilibrium.

Two bottles of gin couldn't be more definite. The number *two* lets us know how purposeful the father is: he is going to drink himself to death. Frequently, people think that alcohol softens or disguises the drinker's life, but just as often it allows the drinker to feel, to unlock emotions that have been shut away out of fear. This idea makes sense of the first line of the poem. The *globe of fear* is a response to the world—sheer terror—that can be released by the gin. How the father actually dies is mysterious, but it seems to me that he has a stroke during which the town of his body achieves *a new equilibrium*. The father is finally in balance. If you are the poet and the man is your father, that is a heartbreaking line to have to write. The terror and vulnerability anyone would feel force Ondaatje back a step.

A brittle tone, a kind of confidential distance, invades the next stanza. *His early life was a terrifying comedy*, Ondaatje writes, *and my mother divorced him again and again.* The speaker relates his story with an air of judgment, holding himself, and by extension us, away from the center of the ludicrous episode of his father's *instant fame*, where, *by falling/dead drunk onto the street*, the man appears to have performed a political act—*which was seen as a crucial/turning point in the Home Rule Movement*. It was probably a turning point in the rules at their home as well.

The humiliation of his so-called political act is that the act wasn't intentional at all; he had fallen down, unconscious. Letters are all about consciousness. Because they are directly addressed to an individual, they are artfully formed expressly for their intended recipient. Intention and execution are exactly what drink won't allow. Though Komunyakaa's father can't write, he communicates with his son. Ondaatje's literate father is his opposite. This is the first of several times the father falls down prone in the poem. Each time he dives yields a curiously beneficial public result, i.e., Home Rule, or the story of a theatrical salute to a happy couple. The last time he falls, he dies, and this, too, produces the sad but beneficial understanding of the father's hidden life.

But why am I assuming that these writers are writing about their own fathers? Couldn't it all be *fiction?* I make the assumption because of the pure electricity of the currents of emotion in the poems and because poets (even fiction writers who are poets) write poetry to point to emotional or spiritual or intellectual truths through language—through letters—and not through plot or character development or the course of ongoing prose. Perhaps I am hopelessly overidentified with these poems because of my own father. I feel free to be openly subjective at the same time as I spy the grammatical and musical structures that underpin—or overthrow—my whirligigs of interpretation. The enterprise of reading poetry permits us, even requires us, as readers to hold both intuition *and* reasoning as twins in our arms. Our obligation to the poem is to balance the reality of the poet's vocabulary with the force of the reaction it provokes in us.

In both of these poems it is the mother who is articulate. In Komunyakaa's, the mother can write, first of all, and she sends postcards. In Ondaatje's, the father is openly *jealous/at my mother's articulate emotion*. Words are in the female realm. Yet each mother divorces or leaves the father—one who beat his wife, the other who was an alcoholic. Each woman's absence leaves her son both desiring that articulation, which only she could give, yet also identified with the father—tied by a Y chromosome to anger and sympathy and hurt and acts of memorialization. What is a poem but an act of memorialization? *Why* were these poems written? *Who needs* to hear the stories of these men? The same question asked of the self-portrait poems can be posed about these family-portrait poems.

The answer here is that the poets need to tell us. They make confidants of us. And we bother to listen because of the urgency of their voices. After all, falling captive to a voice is part of reading a poem. Both these poets, in turn, have fallen captive to their fathers' voices, Komunyakaa to the voice that dictates the letters, *Love, Baby, Honey, Please,* and Ondaatje to the voice of the letters themselves. Those letters have *the clarity of architects* and *a clear hand of the most complete empathy/his heart widening and widening and widening/to all manner of change in his children and friends.* In their fathers' articulating voices hide the men's truly lived lives, their lives of feelings and understanding, and it is the life of the voice that the sons elect, which is, of course, the life of the writer. The writing impulse is the best of their fathers. There is no clearer statement about why people choose to become poets than these two poems.

The fact that Ondaatje's father's *mind* was *drowning* foreshadows the next time the father *made the papers.*

Once on the Colombo docks
saying goodby to a recently married couple
my father, jealous
at my mother's articulate emotion,
dove into the waters of the harbour
and swam after the ship waving farewell.
My mother pretending no affiliation
mingled with the crowd back to the hotel.

Once again he made the papers
though this time my mother
with a note to the editor
corrected the report—saying he was drunk
rather than broken hearted at the parting of friends.

The married couple received both editions
of The Ceylon Times *when their ship reached Aden.*

This time the mother refuses to allow a lie to be printed—but was it a lie? Wasn't it a kind of anguish that caused him to dive after the newly married couple, the more than obvious emblem of an open, happy life (perhaps the one he later tried to have with his new wife)? The fact is, he dove into the waters, dove into the midst of things, as writers must do if they are to turn to their audience—us—the hungry readers, with a full report. The married couple received *both editions/of* The Ceylon Times with both stories, overlapping in truth and falsity. Poetry itself can afford such a layering of the truth. In this it exudes a special kind of accuracy that other written arts can't have—the subtlety and complexity that the system of the line provides when it underpins the system of the sentence. I think this is why nobody demands absolute fact or absolute fiction from a poem. The line, because it is musical, is always going for some kind of rhythmic truth. Is there *false* music? Music reflects emotional pulse—it *is* emotional pulse. It cannot betray the emotion it carries except by being flat. The rhythms here are so energetic that there is no possibility of musical lying.

Part of this poem reads like a newspaper, part of it reads like a dream. It is a strange mix of factual clarity and blurred imagery. No wonder the newlyweds get two editions of *The*

Ceylon Times! Everything in the poem exists on two levels. The system of the sentence dominates the whole midsection of the poem with statements like *For 14 years of marriage/each of them claimed he or she/was the injured party*. But the system of the line frames the midsection with dream images, some of them ghastly as in the end, *the length of his body/the blood entering/the empty reservoir of bones*, which takes us back to early haunted lines such as *He hid where he had been that we might lose him/His letters were a room his body scared*, where music and image balance the narrative information.

A poem whose end returns us to the beginning mirrors the realm of the unconscious, where associations often are made in reverse. The last lines of Komunyakaa's and Ondaatje's poems are, respectively, *Redeemed by what he tried to say* and *the blood searching in his head without metaphor*. Imagine—to make a poem in which *metaphor* is the last word! This is the word that insists on a double world—for there is an ordinary world on this side of the metaphor and an extraordinary world on the other side. There is the waking world and the dream world, the fake and the real, the drunk and the sober, but most of all the silent world and the articulated one. "Metaphor" literally means to transfer or to carry, to transport meaning from one realm to the next, one word to the next. Now meaning is carried from one generation to the next—or carried back. Perhaps metaphor itself is circular, each realm circulating into the other, the balance always going back and forth, as father is inside son and

son is inside father—and as that word "art" is inside articulation.

To be an articulate person means to give your experience a blueprint of consciousness, sharpening its boundaries. Articulation provokes the unconscious to conscious
existence, and this energy of thought leads to understanding. It's a comfort to think that inside a word that means "to
communicate superbly" lies the word "art."

Swimming in the murky undercurrents of my family, I
was drawn to words because they seemed like tablets I
could throw in to clarify the water. Words almost fizzed
through my unconscious and made things swim up in my
mind, like sea animals out of a now-bright ocean. Being
able to articulate who and what I was in my working-class
family painfully separated me from my parents even though
they were proud of places I got to through my words.

My dad read only one thing—not the Bible. It was a
monthly magazine, *Popular Mechanics*. About the shape of
the *National Geographic*, with a perfect binding, it lay in our
turquoise-tiled bathroom, a wish list of all my father could
construct, though somehow time slipped away and most
of the projects lay unfinished. Maybe if my dad could have
drawn his dilemmas on wood and sawn out their shapes,
then his life would have become clear to him—as shaping
language eventually clarified mine. But he stacked up beer
cases instead of vocabulary, and I never could help him with
words, the way Yusef Komunyakaa helped his father.

When I first began writing poetry, I fiercely desired to

make poems so lucid that *Popular Mechanics* would con-
sider publishing one. I always thought it would have been
a much better magazine if I could have seen a boxed inset
with a poem in it on one of its pages, not to mention the
fact that my father might have come across it, just as I imagine fathers wearing workboots and fathers wearing wingtips
riding the subway and reading the Poetry in Motion plac-
ards I help choose. When I sent my poems off to literary
magazines, not *Popular Mechanics*, I heard my dad's refrain:
"Getting too big for your britches?" That's what he asked
whenever I used words he thought were too grand or affected. "But I make my poems out of *regular* words!" I
wanted to retort, though that wasn't strictly so. I loved a big
word when it swam up out of the brine toward me, and still
do, though my poems that mean the most to other people,
I have to admit, use very ordinary words, just as my dad
would have wanted.

CHAPTER ELEVEN

Taking a Bite

 ## ASPARAGUS

This afternoon a man leans over
the hard rolls and the curled
butter, and tells me everything: two
women love him, he loves them, what
should he do?

      The sun
sifts down through the imperceptibly
brownish urban air. I'm going to
suffer for this: turn red, get
blisters or else cancer. I eat
asparagus with my fingers, he
plunges into description.
He's at his wit's end, sewed

up in his own frenzy. He has
breadcrumbs in his beard.
                    I wonder
if I should let my hair go grey
so my advice will be better.
I could wrinkle up my eyelids,
look wise. I could get a pet lizard.
You're not crazy, I tell him.
Others have done this. Me, too.
Messy love is better than none,
I guess. I'm no authority
on sane living.

Which is all true
and no help at all, because
this form of love is like the pain
of childbirth: so intense
it's hard to remember afterwards,
or what kind of screams and grimaces
it pushed you into.

The shrimp arrive on their skewers,
the courtyard trees unroll
their yellowy caterpillars,
pollen powders our shoulders.
He wants them both, he relates
tortures, the coffee

arrives, and altogether I am amazed
at his stupidities.

I sit looking at him
with a sort of wonder,
or is it envy?
Listen, I say to him,
you're very lucky.

MARGARET ATWOOD

(b. 1939)

My husband, Mike, and I first came to Toronto as exchange students in high school, falling in love with the Yorkville of 1964 where the young Margaret Atwood may have been reading her poems—though our school group was not allowed to go. Coming from Buffalo, I thought Toronto was unbelievably hip. Its coolness came from the special chill of ironic Canadian humor that usually got exported so fast people thought it was American. The myth was that Canadians were too nice for that kind of irony, but a poet like Margaret Atwood is not nice at all—she's wicked. And so it dawned on me that a poetic voice might speak, deliciously, out of both sides of its mouth. A poem might function on several social levels, just as people have to do when they are pressed into behavior that really doesn't reflect their personalities and thus act more from disguise than true psyche.

Narrative poems often deal in disguise. Unlike lyric poems, in which a single voice sings its song, narrative poems sometimes divide a voice into the social and the personal, and that is what Atwood does as she tells the story of the listener and the listened to that creates her poem "Asparagus." Why use a poem to tell a story when you can write your tale in prose? What is the difference between poetry and prose, if both tell stories? As lyric poetry sings a song, emphasizing the system of the line, narrative poetry uses fictional techniques, emphasizing the system of the sentence—but even so is far from narrative fiction because it still depends on its intertwining three systems. Atwood's witty pas de deux of the sexes locates the difference between prose and poetry in the jagged music of its lines. She marshalls all the techniques of fiction to achieve the punchline of this poem, defining free verse in the process.

As in Komunyakaa's "My Father's Loveletters" or Nelson's "Women's Locker Room," the system of the line in "Asparagus" is irregular, without a consistent pattern of loud and soft (stressed and unstressed) syllables. We call it free verse, opposing it to metered verse, like the poems of Hopkins, Larkin, or Clare. (Sometimes people confuse free verse with blank verse. Blank verse is metered but unrhymed, like most of the lines in Shakespeare's plays.) But free verse almost always has a discernible though irregular pattern to it, such as the faint suggestion of formal patterns beneath Nelson's lines, or the deeply musical opening and closing sections of Ondaatje's "Letters & Other Worlds." But Atwood's poem doesn't seem musical in these ways. It is not at all melodic; in fact, the music is almost atonal. Rather than wrapping the sentence around the line, as is done in deeply melodic poems like Jane Kenyon's "Let Evening Come," Atwood breaks her lines against the normal word order of the sentence, creating strange pauses in syntax that grate slightly against the ear. She introduces the atonality of serious contemporary music into our traditional idea of the line in the poem. Her technique subverts the idea that music supports; here the *un*music supports the fractured, cranky irony of the speaker.

Irony—when we know more than a character in a story knows—has to do with distance. In this poem the distance is the space of a tabletop. The speaker's self-confidence creates a kind of force field of imperturbability, allowing "Asparagus" to work through timing and timed pauses. The stand-up comic's tool that novelists routinely borrow here is kidnapped into poetry's system of music.

> *This afternoon a man leans over*
> *the hard rolls and the curled*
> *butter, and tells me everything: two*
> *women love him, he loves them, what*
> *should he do?*

The minute we read *the hard rolls and the curled/butter* we know we're in a restaurant. Nobody curls butter at home. Or perhaps it's the leaning gesture that first alerts us to restaurant posture. The system of the image puts forth three simple nouns, *afternoon, rolls,* and *butter,* a stage set framing intimate chat across the playing field of a tabletop. The urban restaurant tête-à-tête, with its cover of noise and clatter, replaces the boudoir as a place of intimate listening. Someone—we won't be sure it's a woman till the third and fourth stanzas—listens while a man talks about two other women. Yet the listener also speaks. If the poem were a cartoon, there would be two bubbles over the narrator, a thought bubble and a speech bubble. To whom does the listener address these thoughts so confidentially? To us, the readers, who apprehend the shorthand of the gossipy tone as if we were her pals. Present tense is the verb tense of gossip, and the sentence style of gossip is the run-on: five clauses jammed together in one rolling declaration.

The speaker who's also a listener is both willing and unwilling to hear the man out, is both condescending and sympathetic, not in equal parts. Unlike the speaker in Jane Kenyon's poem, who cherishes a kind of innocence that is reinforced by hymnlike music, Atwood's speaker cherishes experience, which is reinforced by explosions of exasperation, mimicked by the dissonance in the poem's music.

The pause that comes at the end of every line of poetry in Atwood's poem becomes deeper, because, in the absence of a regular beat, free verse emphasizes line breaks. The rhythm of the sentence plays against the line, and the line, in turn, "breaks" the sentence, distorting ordinary word order by putting pauses between words that normally never have pauses between them. The first line break occurs between a preposition, *over,* and its object, *the hard rolls,* inserting a silence where it never occurs in ordinary sentence structure. The next break is between an adjective, *curled,* and the noun it modifies, *butter*—another place we never leave a silence in our usual speech. Nor would we leave a silence between *two* and *women,* where the next line break occurs. Atwood twirls the internal rhythm of the sentence against itself with her lines, making us conscious of the turns in language with a wry twist of the woman's smile as the man begins to impose on her.

Sometimes it's fun just to run a list of the verbs of a stanza to see how they point to meaning, because verbs are the part of speech that drives the system of the sentence. The whole stanza unfurls along this string of verbs: *leans, tells, love, loves, should do.* When you are unsure of meaning in a poem, it is often helpful to isolate a part of speech and list its connected words. Isolating verbs gives you the action; nouns, the places and ideas; modifiers, the emotional ambience.

Atwood uses stanzas like paragraphs, and the second stanza, which is the longest in the poem, is indented in the beginning and middle, with a kind of substanza at the second indentation.

> *The sun*
> *sifts down through the imperceptibly*
> *brownish urban air. I'm going to*
> *suffer for this: turn red, get*
> *blisters or else cancer. I eat*
> *asparagus with my fingers, he*
> *plunges into description.*
> *He's at his wit's end, sewed*
> *up in his own frenzy. He has*
> *breadcrumbs in his beard.*

Set off by itself, *The sun* takes center stage. It is a paradox of poetry that short lines go slow and longer lines much faster, especially if they contain polysyllabic words like *imperceptibly* in which the unstressed and stressed syllables, attached to one another, move by rapidly. The drastic change in rhythm between the first and second lines is due to the line break, which twists the sentence. There's a big, big silence after the subject, *The sun*, and then the predicate follows, *sifts down through the imperceptibly*—normally we rarely pause between a subject and a verb.

As Atwood makes us hyperaware of language, we become hyperaware of behavior, even as the speaker of the poem does when she says, *I'm going to/suffer for this: turn red, get/blisters or else cancer.* She's aware that she's beleaguered, and she takes action: she eats. Asparagus, a phallic food, is her defense against his onslaught. Food is her armor, and she doesn't even bother with a fork. *I eat/asparagus with my fingers, he/plunges into description.* One of the reasons we are ironically amused is that the line breaks make silences between verb and object, *eat* and *asparagus,* and between subject and verb, *he* and *plunges,* that are never present in spoken speech. Jack Benny used beats of silence in this way for comic effect. Sometimes you can also hear that beat of silence in a Seinfeld routine. Normal sentences work on expectation. When the expectation is slightly changed, the perspective goes askew, and the result can be funny.

Atwood continues to trump expectation in the next few lines. After we hear *He's at his wit's end, sewed/up in his own frenzy* we expect that more frenzy will follow. But instead she steps back and observes, skewing the perspective again with a minute personal detail: *He has/breadcrumbs in his beard.* He has been eating female food, a nice, round breastlike roll with a curl of butter. Their eating habits remind me of a seventeenth-century poem by George Herbert, "Love III." *Love bade me welcome: yet my soul drew back/Guiltie of dust and shine* . . . which ends with these two lines: *You must sit down, sayes Love, and taste my meat:/So I did sit and eat.* Of course the Herbert poem mixes sacred and sexual ideas—there is only a thin membrane between them—while the Atwood poem pits emotional nourishment against sexual hunger; but love has bid both the man and his listener enter, and though the man goes forward, his listener draws back, remembering that she is only desired as an ear, not as a lover, even though she is a sensualist who eats with her hands.

His hair leads to hers, and in part two of the stanza she sets off two words, *I wonder* (incidentally, its stressed syllable, *won-*, rhymes with *sun*, which is set off at the beginning of the stanza). The *I* comes in with a vengeance, sprung from its own cradle of a half line.

> *I wonder*
> *if I should let my hair go grey*
> *so my advice will be better.*
> *I could wrinkle up my eyelids,*
> *look wise. I could get a pet lizard.*

Sublimely bitchy, the speaker sees herself as the wise old witch. Then the visual system of the poem pumps up with a seemingly stray, almost throwaway line, *I could get a pet lizard*. The image of a lizard, grayish, wrinkly skinned, echoes the fake look of wrinkle-eyed wisdom she conjures up. The lizard is lethargic, cold-blooded—that is, picking up the temperature of its surroundings, as the speaker has done. It's as if the lizard speaks the next lines of advice, the first time the speaker addresses the man: *You're not crazy, I tell him./Others have done this. Me too.* These line breaks are perfectly straightforward, completely in sync with the rhythms of normal word order. As she sympathizes with him, rejoining the conversation, the syntax smooths out, and she admits her own culpability. Atwood both distances the woman from the man spilling his guts and allows her to sympathize with him. Suddenly the speaker herself is confessing: *Messy love is better than none,/I guess.* (The beat of comic silence comes in after *none*, the phrase *I guess* half-erasing her statement.) *I'm no authority/on sane living*, the rueful speaker says now, remembering her own passionate attachments, though she brings herself up short in the next stanza with a female pain metaphor, a memory of childbirth, something the man can never experience:

> *Which is all true*
> *and no help at all, because*
> *this form of love is like the pain*
> *of childbirth: so intense*
> *it's hard to remember afterwards,*
> *or what kind of screams and grimaces*
> *it pushed you into.*

She distances her kind of love, *so intense*, from what he feels, comparing her contortions in the act of giving birth to his romantic indecision, her sweat and blood to his restaurant life. Yet because there is no memory of childbirth, there is no memory of *messy love*. Although she overdefines him as a stereotypical dithering male—comedy,

159

of course, depends on overdefinition—she, too, has been there, in the life full of mistakes where *screams and grimaces* are the facial expressions of orgasms as well as of giving birth.

Ambivalent images arrive, the *shrimp* on their *skewers,* the *caterpillars* on their *trees,* the *pollen,* like the *brownish* sunlight in the first stanza, *sifting down.* The fact that the restaurant is serving asparagus lets us know it's spring, and spring is the time for caterpillars and pollen. Yet, because this poem is a song of experience, each image of spring is messy, packed with positives and negatives. The pure image is skewered with the impure thought. The speaker has been skewered by the man, the man has been skewered by his double love, the pollen, that propagating medium of tree sex, has dusted their shoulders, and anyone who has been so dusted knows that pollen stains—you can't get that stuff out. It is just another form of messy love: innocence skewered into experience.

> *The shrimp arrive on their skewers,*
> *the courtyard trees unroll*
> *their yellowy caterpillars,*
> *pollen powders our shoulders.*
> *He wants them both, he relates*
> *tortures, the coffee*
> *arrives, and altogether I am*
> *amazed at his stupidities.*

From this amazement a spirit of ironically rescuing self-consciousness reappears, and the listener feels both *wonder*, at the sheer narrowness of his desire, and *envy*. She's jealous; we, the readers, knew it all along. Who isn't jealous of someone who's in love with two people and wants them both? Isn't that a luxury of excess we wish we had?

> *I sit looking at him*
> *with a sort of wonder,*
> *or is it envy?*
> *Listen, I say to him,*
> *you're very lucky.*

Narrative poetry uses the unfolding of a tale toward a lyric moment, a moment of realization, and usually a moment of wise utterance, a conclusion that feels spoken aloud by the poet, lifting out of the poem at the end. A poem's rhythms drive it to this finale, as May Swenson's "Question" is driven toward its last line, *How will I hide?* Or as Marilyn Nelson's self-portrait pushes toward *and let the woman live.* Poems use the systems of the line, the sentence, and the image to point toward an emotional closure that is so linguistically logical that it seems no other conclusion can be made, even though the last line can come as a surprise, such as Philip Larkin's *Or not untrue and not unkind.* No matter how much narration happens in a shorter poem, the poem still does not develop a plot or full characters. It doesn't have the time—or the interest. Unlike a story's, the poem's trajectory is toward a moment of insight or emotion; it is not, like prose, a development proceeding over time. The point of a story is in its telling, but narration in a poem points to realization, just as Atwood comes to her double-edged conclusion: *Listen, I say to him,/you're very lucky.* Only the stupid are *lucky*, or the innocent. Or those in love.

When the speaker refuses any focus but the cold spotlight of her own jaded eye, she is bent on wisdom. Of course it is wisdom we want from poetry. We pore over poems for their wise words. But here the ironic wisdom comes with the recognition that the stupid are lucky. And the wise? Ah, the wise are listeners.

Poems are often called "timeless," though just as often they depend on a time and place. Inside that restaurant at that table, the relationship of the talker and listener is frozen in time because the listener never shows her hand. She always speaks from behind her ironic screen. This frieze, this freeze, this stillness within a frame combines an unwaveringly cold eye with a warm acceptance of what the eye sees. Underneath it all, there's a little hot spot in this poem: the sensuous pleasure that is keyed by the title, "Asparagus." The listener is a sensualist first, taking in with her eyes and ears and mouth and hands the whole event of the meal as well as the man's angst.

Some years ago, I started keeping what I call The Happy

Diary. That's where, on exasperating days, I write down only the most delightful thing that happened to me. I am shocked to say that often this involves food. There are many days that are not a complete waste because of a curled comma of butter, or a pink question mark of a shrimp, or the exclamation mark of an asparagus. Perhaps, beneath its story, this is a poem about the texture of an afternoon. It's spring in these stanzas, after all. Time to eat with our fingers.

CHAPTER TWELVE

Joy

 FILLING STATION

Oh, but it is dirty!
—this little filling station,
oil-soaked, oil-permeated
to a disturbing, over-all
black translucency.
Be careful with that match!

Father wears a dirty,
oil-soaked monkey suit
that cuts him under the arms,
and several quick and saucy
and greasy sons assist him
(it's a family filling station),
all quite thoroughly dirty.

Do they live in the station?
It has a cement porch
behind the pumps, and on it
a set of crushed and grease-
impregnated wickerwork;
on the wicker sofa
a dirty dog, quite comfy.

Some comic books provide
the only note of color —
of certain color. They lie
upon a big dim doily
draping a taboret
(part of the set), beside
a big hirsute begonia.

Why the extraneous plant?
Why the taboret?
Why, oh why, the doily?
(Embroidered in daisy stitch
with marguerites, I think,
and heavy with gray crochet.)
Somebody embroidered the doily.
Somebody waters the plant,
or oils it, maybe. Somebody
arranges the rows of cans
so that they softly say:

ESSO — SO — SO — SO
to high-strung automobiles.
Somebody loves us all.

ELIZABETH BISHOP

(1911–1979)

When you can't make sense of the world in any other way, merely to describe what you see before you leads to understanding. That is the lesson of the watching way of life, whether you are a detective tailing a suspect, or a bird-watcher, or a child. The clue to the life understood is observation. When Elizabeth Bishop was eight months old, her father died. Her mother's mental breakdowns and eventual institutionalization meant that by the age of five the young Elizabeth was shuttling back and forth between one set of grandparents in New England and the other in Nova Scotia, the beginning of a life in perpetual transit. For this poet, life was a tangle of travel due to mysterious circumstances; she developed a poetic art out of getting her bearings. After all, when you are at a complete loss as to how you came to be where you are, to describe what is before you is the beginning of restoration. This the lesson of fictional sleuths like Miss Jane Marple and Nero Wolfe, of naturalists like John James Audubon and Roger Tory Peterson:

to describe, describe, describe the world, recording scrupulously, and thus also to watch a theory emerge. Description becomes knowledge. Details inform you of the shape of the world. Shape means perspective. If you are in a state of disorientation, you will gain a point of view. A point of view makes a sense of humor possible. And humor not only saves us from confusion, it paradoxically gives us the camera eye we need for sharp description. Not only is Elizabeth Bishop a noticing type of poet, she is funny. Capable of being amused, she amuses us, and it is a joy to read her. Joy is the inadvertent apotheosis of observation. The unexpected result of training your eye on detail is that the world becomes beautiful simply *because* it is noticed, and therefore appreciated. To have a sense of humor in an approving world—there is no fuller definition of enjoying where you are. And here we are with Bishop at a "Filling Station."

> *Oh, but it is dirty!*
> *—this little filling station,*
> *oil-soaked, oil-permeated*
> *to a disturbing, over-all*
> *black translucency.*
> *Be careful with that match!*

Oh, but it is dirty! she exclaims in the present tense. It seems we will be perennially in the filling station, getting gas, liquid nourishment to drive us forward—as vehicles for existence. The present tense, not the future tense, is the tense of forever because it pulses a current of "now" into all activity. *Be careful with that match!* she warns us. Bishop assumes her readers are her traveling companions, and by the end of the first stanza we share the intimacy of fellow travelers, passing through the world as witnesses. (Everything is interesting to observers; they are never bored.) Here we find ourselves at a place that is *oil-soaked, oil-permeated/to a disturbing, over-all/black translucency.*

Bishop revises what she says as she deepens what she sees. At first the station is *oil-soaked,* but then, as she notices more, it's *oil-permeated.* The oil is so embedded it changes the surfaces of things *to a disturbing, over-all/black translucency.* Each stage is ever more carefully scrutinized—and not neutrally. We are Bishop's chosen companions, after all; she claims us as her familiars—the sort of people who would find the oiliness *disturbing*—then pokes us in the ribs with her joke about the match. This is a place to escape from immediately!

Yet observers never escape; they sees things through, instead. (That's the watching way.)

> *Father wears a dirty,*
> *oil-soaked monkey suit*
> *that cuts him under the arms,*
> *and several quick and saucy*
> *and greasy sons assist him*

(it's a family filling station),
all quite thoroughly dirty.

Within two stanzas, she's told us that the place and its inhabitants are *dirty* three times. Why, when the world is so exquisitely detailed, does she insist on that same word over and over again? Reusing the *dirty* word makes us feel that nothing seems to be happening. And so we learn the necessary patience of the watcher. When you are tailing a subject, the subject's world takes a lot of establishing. We have to trust, as Bishop does, that the closer the look, the greater the distance you possess—and the greater possibility for humor. When she says *Father* in her generic way, referring to the owner, we are in her confidence, sharing her point of view, and yet it is a point of view we would never have except for her. She's the one who catches the way his overall *cuts him under the arms,* and how the black gold keeps embedding itself, now in the *oil-soaked monkey suit.* There's that exact phrase, *oil-soaked,* again. With all her discriminating powers, why use it again? Because the return to the phrase, as to the word *dirty,* is a return to the key note. This is not the same as the musical repetition Jane Kenyon uses in "Let Evening Come" (even though all duplication of sound makes some kind of music). Bishop's recapitulation refocuses attention. The describer's eye returns to *clues,* Jane Marple's technique of understanding what happened.

The standard wisdom of the literary detective says that

varied vocabulary is the key to sharp notation; a true scrutinizer rarely repeats. Yet Bishop's repetition is keen because it is reorienting—the way bird-watchers sweep the binoculars to the same tree in order to make sure of their bearings. Once gotten, descriptive precision is necessary again, and that's where Bishop's satisfyingly individual adjectives appear. The man's sons are *several quick and saucy/and greasy*. Those adjectives could be the names for the sons: Several, Quick, Saucy, and Greasy. Jaunty and cartoonish, they stand as if she had outlined them in Magic Marker. After she pokes our ribs (*it's a family filling station*), she purses her lips as her grandmother might have done and spurns the joint: *all quite thoroughly dirty*. Not only does the refocusing on *dirty* reemphasize how grimy the place is, it deepens the judgment of those adverbs *quite thoroughly*. My own grandmother would have pursed her lips in the same way—and at a similar sight. The inescapability of the dirt teases out a question: *Do they live in the station?*

Yes, of course they do, I thought immediately when I first read this poem. My grandfather Gilbert Wright built one of the first gas stations in his part of upstate New York, a jerry-built structure, somewhere between house, store, and garage—and it was all three, presided over by our blind guard dog, Pal. The garage was a mishmash marvel of boxes of Model A parts stacked beneath a farmer's daughter calendar. The store wafted a heaven of smells: the dry sneeze-inducing flour, sugar, and laundry soap, the syrupy smell of root beer,

Coca-Cola, and toffee, the rubbery whiff of windshield-
wiper blades, and the smooth, crude smell of engine oil over
all. The house behind, my grandmother's realm, smelled of
molasses cookies and the starch of the embroidered doilies
on the upright piano and the davenport. My grandmother
Ruth battled the grease and dirt of La Grange Garage till her
dying day; she would have hated Bishop's filling station.

*It has a cement porch
behind the pumps, and on it
a set of crushed and grease-
impregnated wickerwork;
on the wicker sofa
a dirty dog, quite comfy.*

Even though I suffered at first from Bishop's put-down
of the station and the men in it, I soared at the idea that she
wrote the poem at all. That a comfy dog, just like Pal, could
be the subject of a poem made me recognize the value of
this hearty dirtiness. La Grange Garage was an Esso station.

The ambivalence I feel reading this poem comes from
the special conjunction of the facts that my grandparents
shared the same values as Bishop but were in the very circumstances she describes. At first I felt ashamed to have La
Grange Garage belittled, and elated that she also knew about
those spots where filthy happiness prevails. Bishop herself
must have experienced terrible shame at her own back-

ground. Having to tell people that your mother was in a mental hospital couldn't have been easy in 1916—it's difficult to pop into conversation today. Bishop's biographer, Brett Millier, tells us in *Elizabeth Bishop: Life and the Memory of It* that the poet saw her mother only a few times after the mother's breakdown and institutionalization. The story of her mother may have felt to Bishop like a secret too dirty to wash away. Yet as the oil-hyphenated words become doused with grease in the second stanza, and the wicker in the third becomes *grease-impregnated*, we begin to know that this place is so dirty it will never be clean; and this becomes the peculiar source of its happiness.

Often when an ebullient and self-possessed entity saunters into Bishop's poems, it seems to be in the shape of an animal. Toward the end of her life Bishop would write a poem called "Pink Dog," and in that poem would describe a mongrel mother dog at carnival time, out among the revelers. (Bishop lived for many years in Brazil.) When the speaker asks the dog where her babies are, the shadow of Bishop's mother seems to fly through the poem. The hairless pink dog, like a batty bag lady, conveys maternal presence, out among the crazies at carnival. The filling station seems also like a kind of benign nuthouse, where the *dirty dog* is *quite comfy*, right at home. The filling station itself is like a greasy Mardi Gras where everything is upside-down and saucy people can do exactly what they want, the whole scene held perennially in a comic moment.

Some comic books provide
the only note of color —
of certain color. They lie
upon a big dim doily
draping a taboret
(part of the set), beside
a big hirsute begonia.

Part of the watching way of life is watching *again*. Bishop notes, then *renotes* what she studies. *Some comic books provide/the only note of color*, she begins, then qualifies—*of certain color*. The poet models changing her mind, deepening her description, like a bird-watcher, wincing through her binoculars, narrating what she sees at first, second, third, and fourth glances. These lookings entail revisions, modifications, and corrections as the focus sharpens. She sweeps us into the process of observation; we are with her as she checks, then checks again. To us, her readers and intimates, Bishop displays a kind of imperfection because, quite transparently, she lets us see her re-visioning, re-noticing, getting it right.

Bishop doesn't produce a perfect surface of exact word in precise place; she works at correcting, if not mistakes, then the wrongness of immediate impressions. It's not that the comic books are the *only* color, it's that the place is so greasy you can't exactly tell what colors things *really* are. The comic books are placed, as the dog is in its chair, on *a big dim doily*, entirely out of place in this masculine world. It *drap[es] a taboret*. There, on an end table (an end table!) on the porch (a porch?) of a gas station is a doily (!) on which squats a huge, hairy houseplant—*a big hirsute begonia*. That hairy begonia is as fuzzy as Father and his sons. *Hirsute* is my favorite moment in the poem, because the use of this word next to *big*, *dirty*, and *pumps* is just like the appearance of the doily in the gas station to begin with. It is entirely unlikely, as bizarre as the noun *taboret* in this *oil-soaked* place. Now the subject of the poem reveals itself: unlikeliness. Isn't the world made up of peculiarly unlikely things—and isn't this what we have to explain to ourselves? Think of the orphaned Elizabeth explaining to herself why she lives with her grandparents, why others have parents who make a home, but she doesn't.

Unlikelihood always leads to the child's question, Why? And a series of why's composes the next three lines:

> *Why the extraneous plant?*
> *Why the taboret?*
> *Why, oh why, the doily?*
> *(Embroidered in daisy stitch*
> *with marguerites, I think,*
> *and heavy with gray crochet.)*

Each *Why* makes the incongruities all the more obvious, the vocabulary increasingly heightened and intellectualized.

The plant is *extraneous*—a word people use for correcting compositions, not for describing filling stations. And this stanza rhymes *taboret* with *crochet* at the end. The utterly female order (I think of my own grandmother's variegated embroidery floss) against the male dishevelment (and my grandfather's grease-stained coverall and cap) is even a further disjuncture. Why are the yin of the world and its yang the way they are? The demands for understanding pile up and up, even as the descriptive words flood the stanza. Parentheses reappear. And inside them Bishop meditates on the type of embroidery—*daisy stitch/with marguerites, I think*—and the type of edging, *gray crochet*. The dirty and the clean mix up to form the unlikely world.

In forty-one lines, Bishop manages to use every type of punctuation we traditionally have. Punctuation lies entirely in the realm of the system of the sentence. It is what modulates the storyteller's voice; it is what unravels the sentence to our ears and reveals its rhythms. In the first line, she uses the most and the least frequently occurring types of punctuation, a comma and an exclamation point. With breezy confidence, she dares to open the poem with an exclamation, as if she were jotting down a postcard to us. Writing is a lonely art, and no one is lonelier than a writing orphan—or more befriended by an audience. Perhaps we, her future readers, are her imaginary friends.

Immediately after that daring exclamation, Bishop throws on another mark of punctuation before she utters

another word—the dash. Letters and postcards, those vehicles of intimacy, are littered with them. Dashes mark a
special kind of aside (different from the parentheses she
will use three times later in the poem), and she poises a
dash like a magnifying glass in the fourth stanza. In both
cases, the dash ensures a closer look at the world. Though
dashes in a sentence modify perception, they don't alter
tone of voice. What lies on the other side of a dash is
equally important—even though it is separate from the rest
of the syntax. The dash is like the line between yin and
yang in the familiar symbol: ☯. The sentence, like a river,
flows around the island contained within dashes.

On the other hand, parentheses are much more like a
stage whisper, where an actor turns to address us, her audience, in confidence. Inside parentheses Bishop makes her
jokes—*(part of the set)*, she says, raising an eyebrow. Parentheses are like two raised eyebrows set side by side to contain in print the very comment that the eyebrows would
accompany in speech.

Many poets argue that the line stopping gives enough of
a pause without adding a comma, but Bishop punctuates
her poems exactly like prose. The tale she tells—like a dinner table anecdote—requires attention fine-tuned to the
sentence. And so she brings the commas to show how like-
nesses and disparities hinge and attach, or separate and reat-
tach. Semicolons are her great equalizers. Detaching the
link of "and," they maintain the equal importance of the

information on both their sides. The semicolon is like the balancer in the middle of a seesaw. Commas distribute weight, making the seesaw go up and down, allowing the balance to swing back and forth, readjusting always. But semicolons come to a balance point.

In the final stanza, Bishop uses a colon. A mystery is often solved by the words placed after a colon. The colon implies an opening out, a realization. It is used where information leads to understanding, where the clues all add up. And that is exactly what happens in Bishop's last stanza:

> *Somebody embroidered the doily.*
> *Somebody waters the plant,*
> *or oils it, maybe. Somebody*
> *arranges the rows of cans*
> *so that they softly say:*
> *ESSO—SO—SO—SO*
> *to high-strung automobiles.*
> *Somebody loves us all.*

When *the rows of cans/. . . softly say:/ESSO—SO—SO—SO/to high-strung automobiles*, a newly resolved voice enters the poem. The whispery *ss*'s of the cans, as carefully arranged as lines on a page, are artfully revealed as the answer to the way one goes about living a life—in search of what we will find on the other side of a conjunction, *so*, which means therefore and also is the first syllable of *Some-*

body with a capital S. Here is the joining, the annealing conjunction of Jane Kenyon's "Let Evening Come," after which materializes . . . the name of God, the comforter. After Bishop's three *so*'s the Somebody who acts like God enters the poem. God is an arranger, like an artist, and positions the world. Somebody is the prime mover of a domestic life, the godly person who *waters the plant* and *arranges the rows of cans* and, finally, is the one who *loves us all*.

A comforting hand seems to be on Bishop's forehead, perhaps uttering Jane Kenyon's words *don't be afraid*. Bishop's hands, in turn, are on either side of her reader's head, turning it, directing our gaze. The reward of description—the tactic of noticing details when nothing in the world makes sense—is lucidity. As intelligibility comes from specifics, so does humor. Humor never exists *in general*. It is present only *in details*. And Bishop's saving humor is also godly. It emanates from an oil can that mutters *so* what? There's a *Somebody*, like a huge grandmother in the sky, who's looking out for us. And make no mistake, it's our own inner motors that make us high-strung automobiles.

So, whatever is bothering you doesn't matter. Whatever it is, is OK. Kick down your motor. Somebody loves us all. Bishop's gesture is so complete it traces a kind of circle, like the letter of the alphabet in the middle of jOy.

CHAPTER THIRTEEN

The Shimmering Verge: A Coda

 ### THE FARE

Bury me in my pink pantsuit you said—and I did.
But I'd never dressed you before! I saw the glint
of gold in your jewelry drawer and popped
the earrings in a plastic bag along with pearls,
a pink-and-gold pin, and your perfume. ("What's this?"
the mortician said . . . "Oh well, we'll spray some on.")
Now your words from the coffin: "Take my earrings off!
I've had them on all day, for God's sake!"
You've had them on five days. The lid's closed,
and the sharp stab of a femininity
you couldn't stand for more than two hours in life
is eternal—you'll never relax. I'm 400 miles away.
Should I call up the funeral home and have them removed?
You're not buried yet—stored till the ground thaws—

where, I didn't ask. Probably the mortician's garage.
I should have buried you in slippers and a bathrobe.
Instead, I gave them your shoes. Oh, please,
do it for me. I can't stand the thought of you
pained by vanity forever. Reach your cold hand
up to your ear and pull and hear the click
of the clasp hinge unclasping, then reach
across your face and get the other one
and—this effort could take you days, I know,
since you're dead. Let it be your last effort:
to change my mistake, and be dead in comfort.
Lower your hands in their places
on your low mound of stomach and rest, rest,
you can let go. They'll fall
to the bottom of the casket like tokens,
return fare fallen to the pit
of a coat's satin pocket.

MOLLY PEACOCK

(b. 1947)

Like many girls, I memorized my mother's body all my
life and can picture it in a way that I can hardly picture my own. Similarly, I can see the poems of my literary
mothers—and fathers, uncles, aunts, cousins, sisters, and

brothers, too—much more clearly than poems I've written myself. Yet in the way that I notice the ghost of my mother's hand in my own, I can glimpse the literary family resemblance to my talismans in my own poem "The Fare."

One thing I could do for my mother was make her laugh. She loved seeing the humor in turns of events—even in death, perhaps especially there. I like to think that the opening of "The Fare" would amuse her. I have no material evidence of hearing from her from beyond the grave except once. A few years after her death, I was aiming to put away a watercolor portrait of her in her favorite suit, thinking to exorcise my mother from that particular wall of my life. When I removed the painting, a big box of my stationery way across the room leapt of its own accord off a shelf and scattered a thousand sheets of my name and address all over the floor with a loud, indignant clap. My mother's name, Polly Peacock, was only one letter away from mine. (You could say I came into the world as a rhyming couplet.) "Oh, for Christ's sake, Polly," I said out loud, then asked a question out of May Swenson, "You mean there's vanity in heaven?" My mother, who adored how she looked in that '40s suit, was simply silent. So I came to know there is vanity in heaven, just as I know for sure there's guilt on earth.

All my life, what I've hoped to create in my poems is a complex world, one that accommodates ambivalence, ambiguity, adulthood. For me, ambiguity is that shimmering verge, a phrase I have used throughout this book to describe the components of the complex emotional states we all experience that too often boil down to single words in single categories. Thus death is . . . Supply the predictable adjective: *serious.* How can death be funny? Like the place where one color moves into the next category on a color wheel— is it blue? Or is it green? Is it mallard green? Or is it peacock blue?—each category of experience shimmers into its vergence with the next. Dying itself is a shimmering verge between life and death. For me, poetry always takes place in the verge, and verges always shimmer because the light of the mind shines on both categories at once, trying to distinguish between them.

Marianne Moore, in her poem "The Mind Is an Enchanting Thing," says that the mind *is an enchanted thing/like the glaze on a/katydid-wing/subdivided by sun/till the nettings are legion.* In infinite subdivisions, like sunlight glancing off an insect's wings, ideas for poems arise. "The Fare" arose from the verge between funny and serious, between the afterlife and the time just after death. It sounds almost as sacrilegious to call Elizabeth Bishop "Mom" as it is to make jokes about where they store bodies when the ground's too hard to dig, but it's Bishop who taught me to make those jokes, instructing me to ground them in the soil of description: *pink pantsuit, pink-and-gold pin, perfume, slippers and a bathrobe, a mortician's garage,* a little bit like a filling station. . . . Again, I think of her poem "Pink Dog" and of the mongrel mother dog who risks the hurly-burly of carnival to undertake her doggy mission. I think of that pinkness, and mothers . . .

. . . and the letter P. My mother, who was christened Pauline Wright, felt that marriage gave her a ridiculous name: Polly Peacock—a squawk of a name just short of a bird's shriek. When I see the quantity of "p"s in the opening of "The Fare" (*pink pantsuit, popped, plastic, pearls, pink-and-gold pin, perfume*) I think of a comic version of Anglo-Saxon alliteration—and at the same time admire the courage for expressing complex emotion that the Anonymous poet gives all her readers. I borrow bravery from her and put the *fastness* of the *fens* in the *click of the clasp hinge unclasping*. In my twenties I was fascinated by Anglo-Saxon, Celtic, and Nordic jewelry and in particular by the great enameled purse clasp from the Sutton Hoo treasures. Their preservation, of course, is a long way from jewelry in a Ziploc bag . . . but I take a certain fascinated comfort in the fact that she wrote of her time, and I borrow her mettle to write of mine. With Anonymous as a distant mother, I can try to say what I mean—even though my own mother often did not.

The darkness and guilt of this poem, as well as the alliterative zest and the imploring speech, I have from a Father, Gerard Manley Hopkins, a Jesuit priest as far from my dad as I can imagine, who shows in poem after poem what it means to speak to the beyond. "The Fare" breaks in half with my favorite word, made from my favorite letter of the alphabet, *Oh*. The O of recognition, of orgasm, the facing of what we suddenly have to admit is the shocking reality of a single moment. *Oh* points to the moment as we experience it, without past or future impinging on its nowness. *Oh* heralds genuine emotion, the feeling underneath all other feelings, surfacing with the thrill of a dolphin as it arches above water always made bluer by the arc of its presence. When I address my mother directly, *Oh, please do it for me,* I sometimes hear the anonymous Anglo-Saxon voice addressing Eadwacer, through a thousand years. Back a thousand years on the other side of the world, there is Great-aunt Li Ch'ing-chao, who taught me that discussions of female vanity (which in her case meant female identity and survival) not only belonged in a poem, but were the substance of its life. *Jewelry* and *perfume,* tight *shoes, bathrobes,* and most of all *earrings* that pinch come from Li Ch'ing-chao's sensuous assertion of the female body and the requirements of its adornments. I imagine the poet's painted cheeks and lips and see the makeup on my mother's face in the casket and ask my mother to move, not in the way of the living but in the way I suddenly imagine the dead may be able to move, as my mother materializes—or dematerializes—into the ghost she will become for me.

> *Oh, please,*
> *do it for me. I can't stand the thought of you*
> *pained by vanity forever. Reach your cold hand*
> *up to your ear and pull and hear the click*
> *of the clasp hinge unclasping, then reach*
> *across your face and get the other one*

and—this effort could take you days, I know,
since you're dead. Let it be your last effort:
to change my mistake, and be dead in comfort.

I hear that word, *comfort*, both in Jane Kenyon's poem and in Gerard Manley Hopkins' cry *where is your comforting?* and I hear Kenyon's *Let* as well. This initially playful poem that talks about my inability to conceive of my mother without a living body (right down to handing her perfume to the mortician—absolutely true, and true to what he said) turns toward the dread of making a hideously permanent mistake, and ultimately toward not being able to let my mother go, even as I instruct her to drop the earrings, to *let go*—there's another of Kenyon's *Let*s.

The tokens at the end of the poem date it, surprisingly. Somehow I had never thought of subway tokens vanishing, dematerializing, being replaced by those slenderly elegant ghosts of money, swipe cards. As one of the poets who choose the poems for Poetry in Motion on the New York City subways, and now on subways in other cities across North America, I am always aware of subway trains and the going underground, to a kind of urban Hades, the place of the dead, where coins must be given if we are to be ferried across the river Styx, where the dead come home. And these tokens in the shape of earrings are what ensure both safe passage and return. No doubt someone will be making earrings out of subway tokens, just as vendors sell earrings made from ancient Chinese coins.

A life beyond . . . that is the life of poetry, and the cycle of life that poems connect us to. This is a less formal poem than many I've written—I poured it out on the page using a big line often with six beats, rushing to speak, and at the end, used a line that shrinks to half the size of the long lines at the beginning, to a mere three beats, a closing down. I never do get to the two syllables of "good-bye." My final image is of that pocket—a place for safekeeping, for money, for the Kleenexes I required to write the poem. Often when we pocket a temporary treasure, it comes back to surprise us when we don the clothing again, discovering what we absently stowed. And a poem is a kind of pocket, after all—a satin one. In real life the satin pocket belonged to the only cashmere coat I ever owned, black and long and angular as the coat of Miss Clavell in Ludwig Bemelmans' *Madeline*. I stood many mornings in it, clicking tokens together in its soft lining, jittering impatiently for the train to come to take me to work, to teach poetry to children, a job of which my mother unmitigatedly approved. Perhaps poetry *is* both the silk purse and the sow's ear. It requires us to hear in its musical system, to see from its imagery, to know from its sentences that we always inhabit a place of overlapping emotions, the place where the shine in your eyes is from tears and those tears come from *both* laughing and crying, the shimmering verge.

CHAPTER FOURTEEN

How to Start a Poetry Circle

. . . *Only Three Rules* . . .

Poetry circles are a guilty pleasure. They can be big or small, public or intimate, with food or without it, with friends or strangers, scheduled casually or planned eons ahead—it really depends on your taste for the circumstances of your mental pleasures. Poetry circles range in intensity and duration from a brief affair to a marriage that lasts. Each has its own brand of passion. The entire point of a poetry circle is to read and talk about poetry, and to make you actually anticipate the time to do this oddball thing that is a supreme breathing exercise without a weight room, a word trove in the presence of things that leave you speechless. Conquering book lists, jostling for attention because you'd better look smart, slumping your shoulders because you feel so stupid, cooking for a crowd, cramming a schedule all are out. All those things are inimical to poetry circles, which are divinely slow in a hurtling world, heavenly in their absence of social, philosophical, and psychological pressure, and, best of all, thrilling in their presence of revelation. Poetry circles make you know you have a soul, and that other people do, too.

Like the three systems for understanding any poem, there are only three rules for organizing any poetry circle:

1. Start small.
The last thing you need in your life is another burden. Three or four people are fine, at first.

2. Share the responsibility.
The last thing you need is to pit a hunger for revelation against a To Do list. Let your local bookstore, library, or poetry organization help. Or join the Poetry Society of America's National Network of Poetry Circles (1-888-USA-POEM; www.poetrysociety.org) and let them be your guide.

3. Limit the frequency.
The last thing you need to do is trade two hours of delicious multiple paradoxes for schedule slavery. In most cases, monthly or seasonal meetings work best.

. . . *The National Network of Poetry Circles* . . .

The National Network of Poetry Circles, brainchild of the Poetry Society of America (the people who bring you *Poetry in Motion*™ on the nation's subways and buses), offers a start-up packet for monthly circles, with book-per-month recommendations and links to people in your area. They will even connect you with a poet whom you might ask to visit your group. Reading the book of a poet who is actually present to answer your questions is like having access to a living handbook—the body of the poem can literally burst forth in your presence.

Belonging to the National Network of Poetry Circles also lets you contact people reading poetry across the country. You can move from one group to another or participate in chat rooms designed only for specific circles. Some circles are small; some are bigger. Some members become fast friends; some are strictly poetry reading partners, limited. If you are timid about organizing—or tired of it—the ready-made poetry circle releases you from having to do anything except come into the presence of poetry a dozen heavenly times a year.

Local libraries and bookstores are natural meeting places; sometimes a school, church, synagogue, or Y will be happy to host. Handing the list to your local bookseller will allow the store to order in advance and have the copies waiting. If you meet in a bookstore, you can purchase the book for the following month at the current month's meeting, but if you meet at a library or other host locale, often a bookseller is happy to come and bring books to sell there. The Academy of American Poets has a book-ordering service, their Poetry Book Club, as does Spring Church Books, a mail-order poetry list in Pennsylvania. On-line bookstores are also happy to accommodate lists of books and dates of meetings. But many groups find that their best friend is the local independent bookseller. The bookseller, familiar with the people in the group, can often make the perfect recommendation. Independent book-sellers also often host poetry readings, and can hook up poetry circles with writers. The Poetry Society of America facilitates all these connections through the National Network of Poetry Circles.

Picking a certain day of a certain week of the month (for instance, the last Wednesday of every month) gets everyone into the circle habit simply and easily. It's nice to know that habit has a Latin root, *habere*, meaning "to have." That regular date lodges comfortably in members' minds—and their schedules. Groups usually meet for an hour and a half to two hours. This is an intense activity—an hour is enough to get wound up, but you need time to follow thoughts through and wind down, too.

Picking the books of poems makes a quandary for people who really want a personal journey through poetry, not an academic course. As well as relying on your bookseller, why not use recommendations from poetry organizations and poets themselves? Chapter 15 provides a list of talisman-poem recommendations from many distinguished poets.

But once you've made a selection, what do you actually talk about? The *whole* book? In two measly hours? I find that it's best to pick two poems to start with. One poem might take you the whole time, or one might lead to the other. What often happens is that you discover how that poem relates to others in the book, and so many correspondences bloom that you do end up with a sense of the book as a whole. Poetry volumes are slim, their paper crisp and sensuous, their typography enticing, and the whole object physically encompassable. While it is an adventure to read a book of poems in sequence from first to last page, discovering the secret order the poet had in mind, most poetry readers are, frankly, grazers. They are superstitious, too, poising their fingers above a book and letting them come down on a page as if it were a passage from the Bible or instructions from the I Ching. You never know what's going to catch your finger—or your eye. You needn't ever be comprehensive about a book of poetry. Sometimes a passionate reading of one poem will last you all month. There is a real difference between being guilty and indulging in a guilty pleasure. A poetry circle never need be guilty. The fiction writer Elizabeth Bowen called guilt "the useless emotion," and as far as dictating the method of reading a poem, it certainly is.

. . . The Slip-in Circle . . .

If you are already in a book club that meets on a regular schedule, you know the horrible homework feeling of having to slog through six hundred pages of a tome you'd never have chosen, but you know that you try to do it out of loyalty to that great paradigmatic book club in the sky. A solution is to slip in a book of poetry, forming a Slip-In Poetry Circle. Since your book club is probably already connected to a bookseller, your regular ordering procedure should make the slip-in a breeze.

I have this heretical news as well: you don't even have to read it in advance. What!? Of course, in an ideal world it is always better to glide elegantly into one's book club beautifully prepared, but the fact is most of us are lucky if we zip in at the last minute wearing matching socks. To get together in a group and wrestle with language, caressing sounds, poking sentences, and petting the ears of images is a divinely unusual activity, and it can be done intensely with immediate concentration. Let the two hours lie open before you; you might as well luxuriate while you have the chance.

. . . *A Seasonal Circle* . . .

From hyacinths and strawberries to cranberries and pine, poetry connects so naturally to seasons that a simple homemade model for getting together is the Seasonal Circle. Meeting at each equinox and solstice, the Seasonal Circle becomes a ceremony that every member looks forward to. Four times a year is never burdensome, and depending on the number in the group (it may always fluctuate), you may escape hosting one for years. Because there is a pleasantly infrequent formality to this quartet of meetings, getting together at members' homes seems logical. My own book group in London, Ontario, began seasonally. We were four women, in four seasons, choosing four books, each of us hosting one meal, which, because of our work schedules, turned out to be winter breakfast, spring and summer lunches, and a fall evening meal. For us, seasonal food infuses the literary choices (why not eat asparagus as you read Margaret Atwood's "Asparagus"?), but that reflects our ideas of atmosphere, and it depends on how much time we have. After all, you don't have to steam your own dumplings to read Li Ch'ing-chao. In a small group such as this, one person picks one book per season, and that person contacts the local bookstore to order books as soon as possible after the most recent meeting to give everyone ample time to read. We try to separate the choice of book and the book order from the hosting of the meeting in the interest of the low-burden philosophy that has kept us all together.

The Seasonal Circle works for a larger group, too, but a yearly selection committee of three or four needs to guide the orbit of the homemade circle. That's when more co-ordination with a local bookstore and perhaps a connection with the National Network of Poetry Circles might come in. This can make the choices manageable. The idea is to have a circle, but avoid the troublesome O-word, "over-whelmed." The bigger seasonal groups operate just fine with potluck delicacies (also happily achieved with takeout). Everybody brings themselves, a bit of finger food to share, and the book, which will probably be monogrammed with grease prints by the end of a couple of hours. Homemade groups usually meet for two to three hours just because at home we're sloppier with time. You need time to get settled and time to clean up and, crucially, time for the heart of the circle, the talk about language, to sift, to clarify, and to illu-mine a poem's feelings and thoughts.

. . . Secret Circles . . .

Many poetry circles have thrived quietly on their own for decades. A circle in Westchester, New York, has flourished for years in seasonal meetings with nearly forty members and an invited poet each time, whom they now videotape, passing the tape on to cable TV. In Sanibel,

Florida, poetry-reading groups seem to coalesce and disperse with the tides. In London, Ontario, a poetry circle has met every single week(!) for years with what is now a large floating membership—few of whom are particularly literary types. But they are all people who recognize that being deeply affected by language becomes a means to the deeply lived life. Legend has it that long ago Ida Stabler started this group. Ms. Stabler is now in a retirement home—where, incidentally, she has begun another poetry circle. *Our London group*, she writes, *began when, after Friends Meeting . . . one Sunday, I talked with C. . . . Her eyes lighted up & I knew we would get started. Who else? I contacted each of the others, sort of subconsciously feeling each would be interested. It was as simple as that.*

As simple as that, a group of people began to share a secret of the life well lived. And so this must also be in Maine, Montana, Alaska, in New Brunswick, Manitoba, Alberta, and wherever people know that dense language shared means that experience is exalted, and understood.

One summer at the Frost Place in New Hampshire, I looked at all the participants busily talking about poetry and wondered how they would keep up the pulse of their excitement once they returned home. They sure won't do it in their poetry-writing workshops, I thought dully, knowing that writing workshops, even the best of them, are sources of anxiety for any participant. Holding their poems as armor against the crabby pokings of other people's aesthetics, they went to their writing workshops braced to deal with everything but poetry itself. If I could give these people anything, I thought as I prepared my lecture for the next morning, it would be a way to return to the love of poetry that brought them to this mountain farm. Then I slid my notes on "how to write" to the back of my pad and thought instead about what might bring people to gather, not to quake in the face of judgment but to bask in poetry's allure. I pictured a group of people experiencing the slow thrill of language as it flowers in the time-lapse camera of careful reading. I thought of them sorting out their responses and confusions . . . and the surprising queries that would inevitably invigorate them all.

The next morning I walked through the wet grass up to Frost's barn with the image of the poetry circle that had materialized the night before. Climbing up to the podium, I decided to give my lecture not on how to write but on how to read a poem . . . and start a poetry circle. I was as excited as a child—imagine, to return pleasure to a love that had become tattered by criticism and delusion! There in the audience, brows furrowed over pencils raised for furious note taking, were faces that immediately freshened when they, too, saw a clear way to return to their first embrace of poetry. Together we were about to reenter a whole way of life, where words exude both clarity and mystery at once, but this time our experience would be rounder, more voluptuous, because of the circle we were about to draw.

CHAPTER FIFTEEN

Picks for
Poetry Circles

How do you get started poetry shopping? The answer is to browse. Try *not* to be methodical as you cruise the bookstore shelves and the on-line lists. Go for what your senses find appealing—the shapes of poems on pages, the feel of a book, the lure of an opening line or a last line, the titles in the table of contents . . . let your instincts find you a poem and a poet. If you don't try to be comprehensive, you won't be apprehensive.

As a peripatetic poetry shopper, I use tactile, intuitive ways to buy a book that appeals to me. I rely on friends' and booksellers' recommendations, on-line reviews—and impulse. I usually buy anthologies to introduce myself to unfamiliar poets. Though anthologies are nice to have around for standard references, they're not the real, divinely slender thing a book of poems is. Would you ever buy an anthology containing five pages each of several hundred novels?

The way you shop for fiction and nonfiction books—wandering through display tables or glancing at reviews—won't get you very far in finding poetry, because new poetry is infrequently reviewed and old poetry is rarely displayed at the front of the store. Take this as a boon, a special virtue of the art of discovering poetry. You're on your own, but you can certainly take the compass of others with you. You can use the National Network of Poetry Circles' monthly suggestions to guide you, or you can look at the list that follows.

This list consists of talismans recommended for poetry circles by a variety of poets with a variety of tastes. When I contacted some of these poets by phone, each responded within seconds with a choice, even though I told them they had time to think it over. Instinctively, and with alacrity, they knew the poem they would give you—yes, you, a member of the ever-widening circle of poetry readers. The poets' enthusiasms for their choices are personal, excitable, historical, quirky, contemporary, and unpredictable. You just don't know a talisman until it has revealed its name.

. . . Poets' Talismans . . .

Each contributing poet is identified, in parentheses, by the title and publisher of one of his or her recent books. Talisman-poem recommendations are on the indented line following the poet's name. Surprisingly, the poets' choices create crosscurrents among them, and for this reason I have not edited out repetitions or the places where, quite independently, some of the poets recommended one another. Because of the nature of intuitive choices, the list does not pretend to be comprehensive.

AGA SHAHID ALI (*The Country Without a Post Office*, W. W. Norton and Company)
John Milton, "Lycidas"

CHARLES BERNSTEIN (*My Way: Speeches and Poems*, University of Chicago Press)
Gertrude Stein, "Tender Buttons"

ROBERT BLY (*Morning Poems*, HarperCollins)
Pablo Neruda, "Walking Around"

MICHELLE BOISSEAU (*Understory*, Northeastern University Press)
John Keats, "To Autumn"

LUCIE BROCK-BROIDO (*The Master Letters*, Alfred A. Knopf)
Thomas James, "Mummy of a Lady Named Jemutesonekh"

RAFAEL CAMPO (*Diva*, Duke University Press)
Emily Dickinson, "As Imperceptibly as Grief," and William Carlos Williams, "Complaint"

MARILYN CHIN (*The Phoenix Gone, The Terrace Empty*, Milkweed Editions)
Walt Whitman, *Song of Myself*, 1855 edition, and any poem from *The Selected Poems of Ju Fu*, translated by David Hinton

BILLY COLLINS (*Picnic, Lightning*, University of Pittsburgh
Press)
Andrew Marvell, "To His Coy Mistress"

TOI DERRICOTTE (*Tender*, W. W. Norton and Company)
Randall Jarrell, "The Death of the Ball Turret Gunner," and
Anonymous (seventeenth century), "There Was a Man of
Double Deed"

CAROL MUSKE DUKES (*An Octave Above Thunder: New
and Selected Poems*, Viking)
Philip Larkin, "The Explosion," or any poem by Louise
Bogan, *The Blue Estuary*

LYNN EMANUEL (*The Dig and Hotel Fiesta*, University of Illi-
nois Press)
Pablo Neruda, "Ode to Watermelon" (translated by Robert
Bly)

ANNIE FINCH (*Eve*, Story Line Press)
Elizabeth Bishop, "The Moose"

DANA GIOIA (*The Gods of Winter*, Graywolf Press)
Edwin Arlington Robinson, "Luke Havergal," and Theodore
Roethke, "My Papa's Waltz"

DIANE GLANCY (*Asylum in the Grasslands*, Moyer Bell)
Jorie Graham, "Thinking"

LOUISE GLÜCK (*Meadowlands*, Ecco)
William Blake, "The Little Black Boy"

JORIE GRAHAM (*The Dream of the Unified Field*, Ecco Press)
Henry Vaughn, "Distraction," Frank O'Hara, "The Day Lady
Died," and Elizabeth Bishop, "The Fish"

DONALD HALL   (*Without*, Houghton Mifflin)
Thomas Hardy, "During Wind and Rain"

RICHARD HOWARD   (*Like Most Revelations*, Pantheon)
Walt Whitman, "The Sleepers"

MARK JARMAN   (*Questions for Ecclesiastes*, Story Line Press)
Sir Walter Ralegh, "Three Things There Be That Prosper Up
Apace," and John Keats, "When I Have Fears That I May
Cease to Be"

LAWRENCE JOSEPH   (*Curriculum Vitae*, Farrar, Straus &
Giroux)
Wallace Stevens, "The Emperor of Ice Cream"

JOHANNA KELLER   (*The Skull*, The Press at Colorado Col-
lege)
Elizabeth Bishop, "Crusoe in England," and Anthony Hecht,
"The Transparent Man"

MILTON KESSLER   (*The Grand Concourse*, State University of
New York Press)
David Ignatow, "Blessing Myself," Charles Reznikoff, "Te
Diem," and Theodore Roethke, "The Waking"

GALWAY KINNELL   (*Imperfect Thirst*, Houghton Mifflin)
Robert Frost, "Home Burial"

CAROLYN KIZER   (*Mermaids in the Basement*, Copper
Canyon Press)
Theodore Roethke, "The Lost Son" or "In a Dark Time," and
any poem by Constantine Cavafy, translated by Edmund
Keeley

ANN LAUTERBACH   (*On a Stair*, Viking)

Lewis Carroll, "Jabberwocky," Emily Dickinson, "After Great Pain, a Formal Feeling Comes," Ezra Pound, "A Virginal," and Sir Thomas Wyatt, "They Flee from Me That Sometime Did Me Seek"

DAVID LEHMAN (*Valentine Place*, Scribners)
Walt Whitman, *Song of Myself*, 1855 edition, and any poem from John Ashbery, *Some Trees*

PHILLIS LEVIN (*The Afterimage*, Copper Beech Press)
Robert Hayden, "Those Winter Sundays," Anthony Hecht, "The Transparent Man," and Wallace Stevens, "Of Mere Being"

J. D. MCCLATCHY (*The Ten Commandments*, Alfred A. Knopf)
W. B. Yeats, "Leda and the Swan," and Robert Frost, "Home Burial"

CYNTHIA MACDONALD (*I Can't Remember*, Alfred A. Knopf)
Robert Frost, "Fire and Ice"

CHARLES MARTIN (*What the Darkness Proposes*, The Johns Hopkins University Press)
Catullus, "Poem 65"

W. S. MERWIN (*The Folding Cliffs*, Alfred A. Knopf)
Thomas Hardy, "Proud Songsters"

SUSAN MONTEZ (*Radio Free Queens*, Braziller)
Jaroslav Siefert, "Letter from Marienbad"

DAVID MURA (*The Colors of Desire*, Anchor)
W. B. Yeats, "Nineteen Hundred and Nineteen"

MARILYN NELSON (*The Fields of Praise*, Louisiana University Press)

Any poem by E.E. Cummings, Langston Hughes, or Edna St. Vincent Millay

KATHLEEN NORRIS (*Little Girls in Church*, University of Pittsburgh Press)

Kate Daniels, "Four Testimonies"

NAOMI SHIHAB NYE (*Fuel*, Boa Editions)

Tomas Transtromer, "Nocturne" (translated by Robert Bly), and Paulette Giles, "Paper Matches"

SHARON OLDS (*The Wellspring*, Alfred A. Knopf)

George Herbert, "Vertue," and Langston Hughes, "Luck"

ALICIA OSTRIKER (*The Crack in Everything*, University of Pittsburgh Press)

Lucille Clifton, "Good Woman," and Sharon Olds, "The Dead and the Living"

ELISE PASCHEN (*Infidelities*, Story Line Press)

Elizabeth Bishop, "In the Waiting Room," and any poem in *Twenty Poems of Anna Akhmatova*, translated by Jane Kenyon

ROBERT PINSKY (*An Explanation of America*, Farrar, Straus & Giroux)

Edwin Arlington Robinson, "Eros Turannos," or any poem by Emily Dickinson

KATHA POLLITT (*Antarctic Traveller*, Alfred A. Knopf)

John Keats, "When I Have Fears"

ANNA RABINOWITZ (*At the Site of Inside Out*, University of Massachusetts Press)

Constantine Cavafy, "Ithaka"

LIAM RECTOR (*American Prodigal*, Story Line Press)

Elizabeth Bishop, "One Art," and T. S. Eliot, "Four Quartets"

PETER SACKS (*Natal Command*, University of Chicago Press)

W. B. Yeats, "The Wild Swans at Coole"

DAVID ST. JOHN (*Study for the World's Body: New & Selected Poems*, HarperCollins)

Norman Dubie, "The Czar's Last Christmas Letter," and Randall Jarrell, "Seele im Raum"

MARY JO SALTER (*A Kiss in Space*, Alfred A. Knopf)

W. H. Auden, "As I Walked Out One Evening"

SONIA SANCHEZ (*Does Your House Have Lions*, Beacon Press)

Margaret Walker, "For My People," and Gwendolyn Brooks, "The Mother"

SAPPHIRE (*Push*, Alfred A. Knopf)

Ai, "The Kid," and Willie Perdomo, "Where I'm From"

NANCY SCHOENBERGER (*Long Like a River*, New York University Press)

Constantine Cavafy, "The Houses of Achilles" (translated by Edmund Keeley)

HARVEY SHAPIRO (*The Selected Poems of Harvey Shapiro*, Wesleyan University Press)

Sir Thomas Wyatt, "They Flee from Me Who Sometime Did Me Seek"

HAL SIROWITZ (*Mother Said*, Crown)

Edgar Lee Masters, "Fletcher McGee" (in *Spoon River Anthology*)

THOMAS SLEIGH   (*The Chain*, University of Chicago Press)
"Walsinghame," attributed to Sir Walter Ralegh

ELIZABETH SPIRES   (*Worldling*, W. W. Norton and Company)
W. B. Yeats, "Among School Children" and "Lapis Lazuli,"
and any poem by Gwen Harwood

GERALD STERN   (*Bread Without Sugar*, W. W. Norton and
Company)
Nazim Hickmet, "About Living"

STEPHANIE STRICKLAND   (*True North*, University of Notre
Dame Press and Eastgate Systems)
Gerard Manley Hopkins, "Spring and Fall: To a Young Child"

DAVID TRINIDAD   (*Answer Song*, Consortium)
Anne Sexton, "Letter Written on a Ferry While Crossing
Long Island Sound," and any poem from *Lunch Poems*, by
Frank O'Hara

CECILIA VICUNA   (*Unravelling Words & the Weaving of Water*,
Graywolf Press)
St. John of the Cross, "La Noche Oscura del Alma" ("The
Dark Night of the Soul," translated by Eliot Weinberger)

ELLEN BRYANT VOIGT   (*Kyrie*, W. W. Norton and Company)
Bridget Pegeen Kelly, "Song," and Philip Levine, "They Feed
They Lion"

RICHARD WILBUR   (*New and Collected Poems*, Harcourt
Brace)
Robert Frost, "After Apple Picking"

CHARLES WRIGHT   (*The World of the Ten Thousand Things*,
Farrar, Straus & Giroux)
Wallace Stevens, "Sunday Morning"

For information on the National Network of Poetry Circles, a program of the Poetry Society of America, call 1-888-USA-POEM or 212-254-9628, or visit the Poetry Society's Web site at www.poetrysociety.org.

ACKNOWLEDGMENTS

Sometimes the smallest books owe the biggest debts of gratitude:

To my editor, Julie Grau, for her humor and finesse at all hours, and to her assistant, Hanya Yanagihara, for her savoir faire, my happy gratitude.

To publisher Susan Petersen, who suggested the idea for this book, and to my agent and friend, Kathleen Anderson, deepest thanks.

To my Canadian editor, Ellen Seligman, and agent, Bruce Westwood, thanks for your watchfulness from above.

Delighted thanks to designers Claire Vaccaro and Carol Devine Carson, to production editor Elizabeth Wagner, and to publicists Sally Rauber and Kelly Heckler.

To Phillis Levin and Frances Richard for their textual suggestions, thank you from the bottom of my heart.

Myriad, manifold thanks to my friends and students as well as to the Poetry Society of America, the Frost Place, the Poetry Center of the 92nd Street Y, the University of Toronto Creative Writing Program, and the Toronto Writing Workshops for the many ideas that spark the chapters of this book. Particularly I wish to thank:

John Barr, Star Black, Susan Boone, Andrea Brown, William Drenttel, Timothy Donnelly, Susan Downe, Barbara Feldon, Ellen Greenfield, Ann Hammond, Joan Handler, Carolyn Hill, Lois Hirshkowitz, Ruth Karp, Johanna Keller, Karl Kirchwey, Dean Kostos, Ann McColl Lindsay, William Louis-Dreyfus, Bruce Meyer, George Minkoff, Karen Neuberg, Georgianna Orsini, Elise Paschen, Peggy Penn, Ellen Rachlin, Thelma Rosner, Libby Scheier, Georgia Shreve, David Simpson, Ida Stabler, Kate Swisher, and Rebecca Wolff.

And to my husband, Michael Groden, thank you, body and soul.

PERMISSIONS

About the Author

MOLLY PEACOCK, the distinguished author of four books of poems, including *Original Love* and *Take Heart*, as well as a memoir, *Paradise, Piece by Piece*, was a founder of the Poetry in Motion™ program and coeditor of the anthology *Poetry in Motion: 100 Poems from the Subways and Buses*. Her poems have appeared in leading journals such as *The New Yorker, The New Republic, The Nation*, and *The Paris Review*. She was president of the Poetry Society of America from 1989 to 1995 and has lectured widely on the techniques of poetry. Currently a Woodrow Wilson fellow and a contributing writer for *Condé Nast House & Garden*, Peacock works one-to-one with emerging poets. She lives in New York City and London, Ontario.